Confirmed in the Spirit

Authors
Sisters of Notre Dame
Chardon, Ohio

LOYOLAPRESS.
A JESUIT MINISTRY

Chicago

Nihil Obstat:
Reverend Douglas Martis, S.T.D.
Censor Deputatus
July 15, 2005

Imprimatur:
Reverend George J. Rassas
Vicar General
Archdiocese of Chicago
July 18, 2005

The Nihil Obstat and Imprimatur are official declarations that a book is free of doctrinal and moral error. No implication is contained therein that those who have granted the Nihil Obstat and Imprimatur agree with the content, purpose, or statements expressed. Nor do they assume any legal responsibility associated with publication.

The Ad Hoc Committee to Oversee the Use of the Catechism, United States Conference of Catholic Bishops, has found this catechetical text, copyright 2007, to be in conformity, as supplemental catechetical material, with the Catechism of the Catholic Church.

ART ACKNOWLEDGMENTS

Courtesy of Beltrame Family: 77

Catholic Relief Services: 36(r)

John Coburn, Asian Christian Art Association: 2

Corbis: 1(b), 24(t), 25, 26, 28, 29, 57(b), 76

The Crosiers/Gene Plaisted, OSC: iii(a,b,c), 7, 10, 13, 16, 18, 19(r), 23, 24(b), 30, 42(r), 62(r), 66, 94, 96

Courtesy of The Archives of the Dominican Sisters of Hawthorne: 75(r)

Diane Eichhold: 19(l)

Getty: iii(d,g), 1(t), 4, 11, 21, 32, 34(t), 39, 41, 43, 45, 46, 47(r), 48, 49(t), 61, 68–69, 71, 78, 99

The J. Paul Getty Museum, Los Angeles © The J. Paul Getty Museum: iii(e), 52

David LaFleur: 87(b), 98

Library of Congress: 6(r), 57(tl), 57(tr)

"St. Paul the Apostle" © 2000 Markell Studios, Inc. Reproductions at www. BridgeBuilding.com: 72

Phil Martin Photography: 6(l), 17, 27, 44, 49(b), 56, 65, 70(l,r), 83, 87(t), 88(all), 89(all), 91, 97, 105

New Mexico State University Art Gallery Collection.: 42(l)

Fourteen Mosaic Stations of the Cross © Our Lady of the Angels Monastery, Inc., Hanceville, Alabama. All Rights Reserved.: 90(all)

© Brother Jerome Pryor, S.J.: 92(tr), 93(t,b)

The Dennis & Phillip Ratner Museum, www.ratnermuseum.com/Photo by Tyler Mallory: 3(l)

Scala / Art Resource, NY: 12

Spaightwood Galleries, Inc. of Upton MA © 2005 Artists Rights Society (ARS), New York / ADAGP, Paris: 22(l)

Susan Tolonen: 5(r4), 20, 67, 74(t)

Copyright Bill Wittman: 36(l), 54, 86(b)

Cover Design: Judine O'Shea
Cover Illustration: Susan Tolonen
Interior Design: Judine O'Shea

ISBN-13: 978-0-8294-2124-8,   ISBN-10: 0-8294-2124-6

For more information related to the English translation of the *Roman Missal, Third Edition,* see www.loyolapress.com/romanmissal.

LOYOLAPRESS.
A JESUIT MINISTRY

3441 N. Ashland Avenue
Chicago, Illinois 60657
(800) 621-1008
www.loyolapress.com

Confirmed in the Spirit

CONTENTS

WELCOME TO CONFIRMED IN THE SPIRIT		iv
CHAPTER 1	Confirmed in the Spirit	1
CHAPTER 2	Confirmed in Discipleship	11
CHAPTER 3	Confirmed in Faith	21
CHAPTER 4	Confirmed in Love	31
CHAPTER 5	Confirmed in Holiness	41
CHAPTER 6	Confirmed in the Church	51
CHAPTER 7	Confirmed in Grace	61
CHAPTER 8	Confirmed in Witness	71
Things Every Catholic Should Know		81
Living Our Faith		81
Celebrating Our Faith		86
Devotions of Our Faith		90
Glossary		94
A Prayer Guide for the Journey		99
Confirmation Novena		105
Index		107

Welcome to Confirmed in the Spirit

On the day of your Baptism, your parents promised to raise you in the faith and to see that the divine life, which God gives you, is kept safe and grows stronger in your heart. They accepted the responsibility of teaching you what it means to be Catholic and to keep God's commandments, as Jesus taught us, by loving God and your neighbor.

At your Baptism the Holy Spirit filled you with gifts and graces to guide you. Since then your parents, sponsors, parish priest, catechists, and other good Christians have helped you to live the life God has intended for you. Through the celebration of the Eucharist, you have strengthened yourself to respond to God's calling. You also have had to be reconciled with God and your neighbor through the Sacrament of Penance. Now you are getting ready to take another step—celebrating the Sacrament of Confirmation.

Confirmed in the Spirit will help you prepare for being strengthened by the Holy Spirit in the Sacrament of Confirmation. You will review many of the truths you have learned, and you will deepen your understanding of how Confirmation is linked to both Baptism and the Eucharist. More importantly, you will consider how the Holy Spirit can help you choose wisely and act responsibly as you learn how to stay tuned to the Spirit's voice and obey it faithfully.

As you journey deeper into this book, you will gain a greater appreciation for what it means to be confirmed in the Spirit. You will come to realize that only the Spirit of Jesus can help you give witness to the Gospel and serve the Kingdom of God. Two thousand years ago Saint Paul wrote about the goals of all Christians and the challenges they face. He spoke about God's call and promise. "Now the one who has prepared us for this very thing is God, who has given us the Spirit as a first installment." (2 Corinthians 5:5)

Confirmed
in the
Spirit

"Let us pray
to our Father
that he will
pour out the
Holy Spirit
to strengthen
his sons and
daughters
with his gifts."

*The Rite of
Confirmation*

Have you ever felt all alone
in the world? Have you ever
faced a difficult situation,
and you didn't know what
to do? Whom did you ask
for help?

The Spirit Is with Us

"If you love me, you will keep my commandments. And I will ask the Father, and he will give you another Advocate to be with you always, the Spirit of truth, which the world cannot accept, because it neither sees nor knows it. But you know it, because it remains with you, and will be in you. I will not leave you orphans."

John 14:15–18

❖ Understanding Scripture

We have been talking about facing difficult situations and needing help. In this Scripture passage Jesus is talking to his apostles after the Last Supper. He is giving them some final words of comfort before his accusers come to arrest him. Naturally the apostles are nervous, and they're wondering what's coming next. Jesus doesn't deny that he is leaving.

The disciples are afraid of being left behind; they will be lost without Jesus. But Jesus tells them he is sending an **Advocate** to help them.

The term *advocate* has a number of meanings. It comes from a Greek word that can mean "lawyer." It can also mean "mediator," "intercessor," "comforter," or "consoler."

Jesus calls on the "Spirit of truth" to be his friends' advocate and remain with them. Jesus offers us the same support. He tells us, "I will not leave you orphans" (John 14:18).

❖ Scripture and You

Facing the challenges of a new day can be scary. You may have to deal with a difficult situation at school. You may be disturbed by the events you see unfolding in the world. With so many problems facing the world and yourself, it's no wonder that you may ask where God is.

You are just like the disciples listening to Jesus. They have been with him for almost three years, and now he is leaving them. They're trying to make sense of what's happening and are wondering what will come next.

Jesus assures the disciples that he won't leave them orphans. He promises to send his Holy Spirit, the third Person of the Trinity, who is God, to always be with them. Jesus makes that same promise to you today.

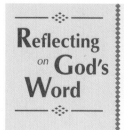

ART Link

This painting by Australian artist John Coburn, entitled *The Last Supper*, depicts Jesus with the disciples in a tropical outdoor setting. Coburn is part of an association of artists from the South Pacific and Asia who wish to express their Christian faith in an Asian context. The message of Jesus continues to take root in a variety of cultures throughout the world.

Reflecting on God's Word

What do you think when you hear Jesus promise not to leave you as an orphan? What problems or concerns can you ask the Holy Spirit to help you handle? Spend a few moments in prayer. Silently talk to God about anything you like.

The Spirit in the Old Testament

Many people think that God really isn't involved in the world, that he simply lets things happen. People see him as being a watchmaker who winds up the world and then steps aside and lets it tick away. The Bible tells a completely different story. It says that from the beginning of Creation, the Spirit of God formed the earth and all of its surroundings, and that God will always be with us.

The word *spirit* in the Old Testament is *ruach,* which can be translated as "wind" or "breath." This is how God's action in Creation is described in the book of Genesis.

God created the heavens and the earth. The earth was a shapeless wasteland, and the heavens were covered with darkness. A mighty wind swept across the waters (adapted from Genesis 1:1–2).

God forms the first man out of the clay of the ground and breathes into him the Spirit of Life (adapted from Genesis 2:7).

The Spirit of God is with his people throughout the Old Testament. With the help of God's Spirit, Moses leads the Hebrew people out of Egypt to freedom. As the Hebrew community grows, God gives his Spirit to the community's leaders (adapted from Numbers 11:17,25).

❖ The Spirit in the New Testament

In the New Testament the Holy Spirit comes to Mary as she answers the call to be the mother of Jesus, the Son of God (Luke 1:35). Jesus is led by the Spirit into the wilderness to pray in Luke 4:1–2. And Jesus reads from the scroll of the prophet Isaiah that the Spirit is upon him as he begins his ministry in Luke 4:16–21.

After Jesus' Resurrection and Ascension, the Holy Spirit comes on Pentecost. In Acts of the Apostles 2:1–4, the Spirit fills the disciples with grace and gives them the courage to proclaim Jesus to the world.

A Popular God

✦ Matt Maher is a popular Christian-rock musician known for singing from the heart and praising God in his work. In his song, "Love Has Come," he sings:

Father, Yahweh, Elohim,
voice of thunder, spirit wind
Breathe on me your very life;
Grace will make the darkness bright.

Chorus: Word of God, enthroned,
dwell in us forevermore;
Love has come to show the way.
Hallelujah, peace be with us
Love has come to show the way.

Make a list of songs, song lyrics, TV shows, movies, or other references to popular culture that remind you of God's presence in the world.

_____

_____

In the World Today

The grace of the Holy Spirit unites us by faith and by our Baptism to the Passion and Resurrection of Christ. The Scripture stories of the Holy Spirit in action are examples of what God has done in the past, but they are also models of how God continues to work in our lives today. The stories are valuable to remember because they help us recognize the work of the Holy Spirit in our own lives. The Spirit is helping us to understand what God is calling us to do. The mission of the Holy Spirit and Jesus are inseparable. Whenever God sends his Son he always sends his Spirit.

The Spirit at Work

✦ Work in groups to prepare a list of ways that you see the Spirit at work in the world today. You can refer to things you have read about, or seen on TV, or you can include things you have observed firsthand.

_____   _____

_____   _____

_____   _____

_____   _____

What is an example of the Holy Spirit helping you in your life?

_____

_____

_____

❖ *Father, Son, and Spirit with Us*

We have been emphasizing that God is not distant from us. He wants us to know how close he is to us. As Jesus said, we are not being left as orphans.

God is our Father, who created the universe from nothing in order to express his love for us. Jesus, God's Son, came to us as Savior and Redeemer, to reunite us with God, to restore the relationship we broke by our sin. Jesus is the visible image of the invisible God. But it is the Holy Spirit who reveals Jesus to us. The Holy Spirit is God alive in the world. The Spirit helps us know we are loved and shows us how to love others.

As we have seen, Jesus sent the Holy Spirit to help, defend, and comfort us. As the Spirit of Truth, the Holy Spirit makes the saving work of Christ present and active in the Church. The Spirit gives us the grace to act for God and others as Jesus did.

The Spirit also helps us become part of a community, called the Body of Christ, or the **Church.** Christ fills the members of this community with the Holy Spirit and builds them, animates them, and sends them to share the Good News with the world.

Images of the Spirit

To help us understand the Holy Spirit, the *Catechism of the Catholic Church* presents a number of images of him. Reflecting on some of these images helps us to think about the Holy Spirit in different ways and to consider what he means to our lives.

❖ Water

Water signifies regeneration and renewal by the Holy Spirit in Baptism, which is necessary for salvation. In the Holy Spirit we are baptized into new life in Christ and become children of God, the Father.

❖ Anointing

Anointing with oil has become so identified with the Holy Spirit that it is almost a synonym for the coming of the Spirit. **Messiah** is the Hebrew word for "anointed one." **Christ** is from Greek and means the same thing. Jesus is the Messiah, the one uniquely "anointed" by the Spirit. Jesus pours out this same Spirit upon us, calling us to be more than we can ever hope to be through our own efforts alone.

❖ Fire

Fire symbolizes the transforming energy of the Holy Spirit. John the Baptist proclaimed that Jesus was the one who would baptize with the Holy Spirit and with fire. We also remember the dramatic events of Pentecost described in the Acts of the Apostles, in which tongues "as of fire" rested on the disciples.

❖ Dove

Think of a dove, a gentle bird, flying to your hand and gently resting on it. In a similar way the Holy Spirit rested on Jesus when he emerged from the waters of his baptism by John. He also gently rests on us and remains with us.

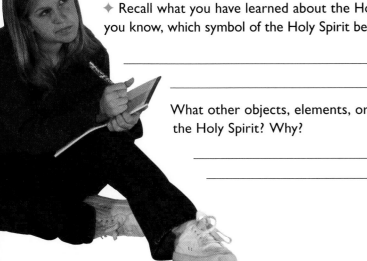

Your Image of the Spirit

✦ Recall what you have learned about the Holy Spirit. Based on what you know, which symbol of the Holy Spirit best relates to your life? Why?

_____

_____

What other objects, elements, or animals could be symbols of the Holy Spirit? Why?

_____

_____

Spirit-Filled People The Spirit's presence has helped Christians of every century to live like Jesus and to become saints. Here is an example of the Holy Spirit at work in Saint Frances Cabrini in New York in 1890.

"No!" The bishop sighed and looked at Mother Frances Cabrini. "No, you do not want the property across the river. There is no drinking water."

"But Bishop," pleaded Frances, never known to give up, "the children in the orphanage need fresh air and a place to run. They can't do it in the crowded house on Fifty-ninth Street."

"Where will you get the money?" the bishop asked impatiently.

"God will take care. Have faith."

The bishop gave in reluctantly. In the next few weeks Frances and her sisters were very busy. They prayed to the Holy Spirit. They went out begging from butchers, bakers, rich friends, and merchants. They got the money, food, and clothing they needed. After they moved in, the land was surveyed and a well was found.

With the guidance of the Spirit, Saint Frances Cabrini was able to help build nearly 70 institutions for the poor and the suffering. She crossed the ocean 30 times to help people in need, proving that nothing stops a Spirit-filled Catholic.

The saints were ordinary Catholics just like you. They relied on the Holy Spirit and followed wherever he led them. ✦

Called to Service

✦ The Spirit gives you strength to help your neighbors just as he gave strength to Frances Cabrini. Write a paragraph explaining how you could help a person or group in need. The paragraph can be about a person or group you know personally, or one you have read or heard about.

_____

_____

_____

_____

_____

_____

A Confirmed Commitment

You are preparing to receive a special outpouring of the Holy Spirit in the Sacrament of Confirmation, an opportunity to deepen your commitment to Jesus and his Church. The grace of the Holy Spirit unites us by faith and by our Baptism to the Passion and Resurrection of Christ. In Confirmation the Holy Spirit brings us closer to Christ, brings us into closer relationship with the Church, and helps us witness to our faith in what we say and what we do. You've heard the phrase "Practice what you preach." Confirmation gives us the strength to practice and act on our beliefs, or to practice what we preach.

❖ *The Spirit Helper*

With which of these thoughts do you identify?

I don't know what to do.

How can I plan to be a better person than I am?

How can I make good choices?

How do I prepare for the future when I don't understand what's happening today?

However uncertain you feel and however many questions you have, the Spirit is always ready to help you. In Confirmation he comes to you in a special way. This gift of the Holy Spirit in Confirmation will help you explore the many questions in your life and will help you live the life to which God calls you.

Comparing Commitments

✦ Just as the Holy Spirit comes to us in Confirmation, we know of Scripture stories that describe his presence in people's lives. Of the stories described on page 3, which best illustrates how the Spirit is active in your life as you prepare to celebrate the Sacrament of Confirmation?

_____

_____

Why?

_____

_____

For Confirmation: Your Christian Name

At your Baptism you were given your Christian name. You may have been named after a relative or a saint or some other person your parents thought would be a good role model for you. As you seal your Baptism in Confirmation, you can keep that name or choose the name of another saint or holy person to be your model of Christian life.

Prayer to the Holy Spirit

Think about how the Spirit guided and inspired people in the Scripture passages you have read. Silently pray this traditional Prayer to the Holy Spirit.

Come, Holy Spirit, fill the hearts of your faithful.

And kindle in them the fire of your love.

Send forth your Spirit and they shall be created.

And you shall renew the face of the earth.

Lord,

by the light of the Holy Spirit

you have taught the hearts of your faithful.

In the same Spirit

help us to relish what is right

and always rejoice in your consolation.

We ask this through Christ our Lord.

Amen.

You have asked the Holy Spirit to be with you always, to fill your heart with his presence. The Spirit renews the face of the earth and renews you in the Sacrament of Confirmation. Silently speak to God and listen as he shares his great love for you.

Summary

Your Special Journal

Keeping a journal will help you enter more deeply into your preparation for Confirmation. In this journal you can keep prayers, new ideas, and any other thoughts or feelings about your experience of preparing for the sacrament. You will be invited to record in your journal specific ways to focus on the themes of each chapter. You may also wish to place in your journal artwork, pictures, or other keepsakes from your preparation for Confirmation. You may be asked to share what you have written in your journal, but no one will read it. Periodically reviewing your journal will allow you to better appreciate and understand God's grace at work in your life as you prepare for Confirmation.

Remember

Who is the Holy Spirit?
The Holy Spirit is our Advocate whom Jesus sent so that we would not be left orphans.

What does the Holy Spirit do?
The Holy Spirit helps us learn what Jesus means to us and gives us the grace to act as Jesus did.

How does the Holy Spirit give meaning to our lives?
The Holy Spirit helps us know we are loved and shows us how to love others.

Words to Know	
Advocate	Church
Christ	Messiah

Respond

Use your journal to enter more deeply into this chapter. Begin with the prayer on page 5 of your journal. Then quietly spend time on journal pages 6–8.

Reach Out

The Old Testament word *ruach* can be translated as "wind" or "breath." Just like our breath, the Spirit flows through us and through all parts of life. Reflect on times when you have felt this presence of the Spirit and name three times you have passed his love on to others.

2. Preparing for Confirmation involves hearing the stories of other Christians. Interview a priest, teacher, parishioner, or family member. Ask this person about people and events that have influenced his or her faith life. Write about it in your journal. (See Your Special Journal section above.)

3. Collect prayers and/or hymns to the Holy Spirit. Report on three new things they reveal to you about the Spirit.

4. Read one of the Old or New Testament stories on page 3. Tell someone about whichever story you choose.

REVIEW

Confirming the Facts

Complete the sentences. If you answer them correctly, the boxed letters will spell *confirmed*.

1. The disciples of Jesus were filled with the Spirit on
— — — — — ☐ — — — .

2. The Holy Spirit gave the disciples
— ☐ — — — — — to proclaim Jesus.

3. The Old Testament word for *spirit* can be
translated as "— — ☐ — " or "breath."

4. Fire symbolizes the
— — — — — ☐ — — — — —
energy of the Spirit.

5. The Holy Spirit rested on Jesus like a dove when
Jesus emerged from the waters of his
— — — — ☐ — — .

6. You receive an
— — — — — — ☐ — — — of the
Holy Spirit in the Sacrament of Confirmation.

7. For Confirmation you can choose the name
of a saint to be your ☐ — — — — of
Christian life.

8. The Spirit
— — — — — — — — — ☐ — — our bond
with the Church in Confirmation.

9. The Holy Spirit is our
☐ — — — — — — , or defender.

The Spirit of Truth

Write T for *true* or F for *false* for the following statements about this chapter. Edit each false answer to make it true.

___ **1.** The Holy Spirit is referred to as the Spirit of Truth in the Gospel of John.

___ **2.** John the Baptist was the advocate whom Jesus promised to send to help the apostles.

___ **3.** *Advocate* can mean "mediator," "intercessor," "comforter," or "consoler."

___ **4.** Jesus promised not to leave the disciples as martyrs.

___ **5.** *Messiah* is the Hebrew word meaning "Son of God."

Confirmation Puzzler

Cross out the first letter and every other one. The remaining letters spell four words that tell what the Spirit is for you. List them.

J	H	E	E	S	L	U	P	S	E
C	R	H	C	R	O	I	N	Y	S
K	O	B	L	N	E	W	R	A	C
Q	O	A	M	P	F	J	O	U	R
B	T	X	E	E	R	K	I	I	N
C	T	V	E	Y	R	D	C	F	E
W	S	U	S	P	O	Z	R		

_____

_____

_____

_____

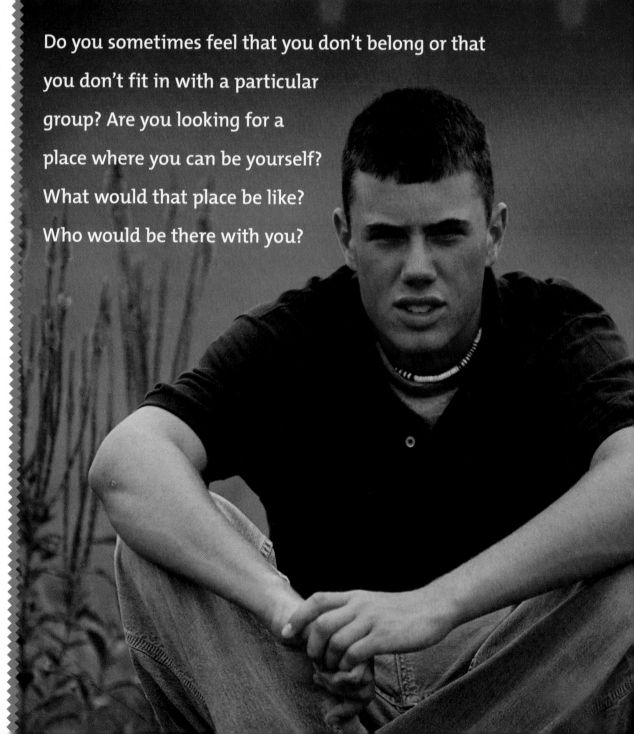

Confirmed in Discipleship

"We ask you Father, with your Son to send the Holy Spirit upon the water of this font. May all who are buried with Christ in the death of Baptism rise also with him to newness of life."

The Rite of Baptism

Do you sometimes feel that you don't belong or that you don't fit in with a particular group? Are you looking for a place where you can be yourself? What would that place be like? Who would be there with you?

Gathered Together as God's People

For I will take you away from among the nations, gather you from all the foreign lands, and bring you back to your own land. I will sprinkle clean water upon you to cleanse you from all your impurities, and from all your idols I will cleanse you. I will give you a new heart and place a new spirit within you, taking from your bodies your stony hearts and giving you natural hearts. I will put my spirit within you and make you live by my statutes, careful to observe my decrees. You shall live in the land I gave your fathers; you shall be my people, and I will be your God.

Ezekiel 36:24–28

❖ *Understanding Scripture*

If you have ever been away from home and felt homesick, you know how lonely and discouraging it can be. The prophet Ezekiel writes to the Israelites, who are living far from home and feeling removed from God.

God had promised to take care of the Israelites if they obeyed him. But because they refused to follow his plan, their Temple in Jerusalem was destroyed and they were forced to live in the distant land of Babylon.

Ezekiel is God's messenger to the Israelites. Through him, God promises the Israelites that they will become his people again. God promises that they will return home. He will wash away their sins and fill their hearts with his Spirit so that they become a new people.

This is the prophet Ezekiel from the Sistine Chapel, which was painted by Michelangelo between 1508 and 1512. It is among the many images in the history of humanity, from Creation to the Last Judgment, that Michelangelo painted. He depicted five prophets from the Old Testament and five prophets, or sibyls, from pagan culture.

❖ *Scripture and You*

Because of original sin we have been born in exile. Like the Israelites, we sometimes choose not to obey God. When we do this we feel far from home and far from the place where God wants us to be. Our human nature is weakened and we are subject to ignorance, suffering, and death. Ezekiel's words remind us that God keeps his promises and is always ready to bring us back to him. He does this for us in the Sacraments of Christian Initiation—Baptism, Confirmation, and the Eucharist.

Reflecting *on* **God's Word**

Take a moment to rest peacefully in God's presence. Hear his words from the prophet Ezekiel spoken directly to you. Of what do you want to be washed clean? What distractions keep you from worshipping God alone? Pray that you will be open to the Holy Spirit so that your heart may be filled with God's love. Thank God for the Spirit he has given you to help you follow his plan. Take a few moments to listen to God and to speak to him about whatever you like.

God Calls a People

God is always inviting us to be part of his family. Like he did with the Israelites, God also made a promise, or covenant, with Abraham and Sarah. He asked them to leave their home and family for a land that he would give them. In return for this sacrifice, God promised that Abraham would become the leader of a great nation of God's people.

Centuries later, God made another covenant. He asked Moses to give his commandments to the Israelites at Mount Sinai. There the Israelites promised to obey God's commandments, and in return, he promised to care for them and be their God.

God made a new covenant with us through Jesus, his Son. At the Last Supper, as described in Luke 22:20, Jesus took a cup of wine and said, "This cup is the new covenant in my blood, which will be shed for you."

By his death and Resurrection Jesus formed a new community. This new community, his Church, was made up of people who believed in him, followed his teaching, and kept his commandment of loving one another. People who follow Jesus are called disciples.

On the festival of Pentecost, God the Father and Jesus his Son sent the Holy Spirit to fill the disciples with the Spirit's grace. The disciples then told the Good News of Jesus to everyone present. Though the people came from different places and spoke many different languages, the power of the Holy Spirit allowed them to understand the disciples in their own languages. That day three thousand people were baptized and received the gift of the Holy Spirit. The Church was alive.

❖ A Spirit-Filled Community

Brought to life and animated by the Spirit, the believers were formed into a community with four characteristics.
- Community—living and praying together; sharing common bonds
- Message—learning from the apostles; proclaiming the Good News
- Worship—praying in the Temple; breaking bread in honor of Jesus
- Service—loving one another; caring for the poor

❖ The Church Blossoms

The Church grew as the word about Jesus spread. People who wanted to belong to the Christian community prepared to enter the Church at the annual celebration of Jesus' death and Resurrection during the Easter Vigil.

These soon-to-be Christians descended into a pool of water to signify dying with Christ and giving up their old way of life. They were baptized "In the name of the Father, and of the Son, and of the Holy Spirit." The bishop laid hands on them and anointed them with oil, confirming, strengthening, and perfecting the Holy Spirit's presence in them. Their initiation was completed when they received the Eucharist for the first time.

Initiation Today

When a baby is born into a family it is a special occasion. In the same way, when someone becomes a member of God's family, the Church welcomes him or her through the Sacraments of Initiation: Baptism, Confirmation, and the Eucharist.

In the Eastern Church Confirmation is administered immediately after an infant is baptized and is followed by participation in the Eucharist. Over the course of time, Confirmation and Eucharist became separated from Baptism in the Western Church. Recently the Western Church has emphasized the unity of the Sacraments of Initiation by bringing back the **Rite of Christian Initiation of Adults (RCIA)**. In this rite adults learn what it means to be a baptized disciple of Jesus—to follow his teachings and to live them every day. Adults are initiated into the Church by celebrating all three sacraments at the Easter Vigil.

Although your celebrations of Baptism, Confirmation, and Eucharist are probably years apart, they are closely related. First of all, they are **sacraments,** efficacious signs of grace given to the Church by Christ. Divine life is given to us through them. The sacraments are the most important signs of the Holy Spirit's presence in your life. They help you realize there is more to life than simply satisfying your own desires. They make present the grace you need to use your time, talent, and energy for the benefit of God and others.

Being a Disciple

◆ Write what it means to you to be a baptized disciple of Jesus.

_____

_____

❖ Baptism

We are learning that the Sacraments of Initiation welcome us into the Church. In Baptism, the first sacrament we celebrate, we are freed from **original sin** and born into new life in Jesus.

Baptism is a sign of God's covenant with us. It's an agreement in which God promises to always be with us and to help us build our relationships with him and others. When we accept this covenant, we promise God that we will try to be like Jesus, his model of what it means to be a person for others.

In addition to forming a covenant between us and God, Baptism makes us an adopted son or daughter of God and a member of the Body of Christ, the Church. Baptism marks us permanently as Christians and allows us to share in the priesthood of Jesus, the common priesthood to which all believers belong. United with him in his priesthood, we exhibit the grace of Baptism in all areas of our life—personal, family, social, and as members of the Church—and live out the call to holiness, which is addressed to all the baptized.

The new life we receive in Baptism is called **sanctifying grace.** This grace takes away original sin; it helps us love God, believe in him, and hope in him. It also helps us follow the directions of the Holy Spirit, which guide us to live the life God has planned for us. If we make the most of this grace, we improve our relationship with him.

Preparing for Confirmation

You are preparing to celebrate Confirmation, the second Sacrament of Initiation. This time of preparation gives you the opportunity to look carefully at the direction of your life. You need to make decisions every day, and the steady stream of difficult choices can be very confusing. This confusion can lead you to question how God is involved in your life or whether he's involved at all.

As we saw in the reading that began this chapter, God wants to renew us, to wash away our sins, and give us hearts full of his Spirit. We will not be alone as we prepare for the difficult decisions of life.

In Confirmation you affirm your baptismal promises. The Sacrament of Confirmation seals your Baptism and reinforces the life-giving gifts you received in Baptism. Confirmation brings you closer to Christ, strengthens the Gifts of the Holy Spirit, unites you more closely to the Church, and helps you to follow Jesus' example in your words and actions.

In Confirmation, as in Baptism, you are marked with a permanent character, or seal. Because of this seal you can only be baptized and confirmed once. Just as you can never stop being someone's brother, sister, or cousin, you can never stop being a child of God once you are baptized.

Participation in the Eucharist completes Christian initiation. Receiving it we continually renew our participation in Christ's saving death and Resurrection. The Eucharist brings us closer to Jesus and others.

The Strength to Follow Jesus

✦ As a disciple, you are called to follow Jesus in your words and actions. This is not an easy task, but the support of your Catholic community can help. In small groups, form a community dedicated to following Jesus, and propose one way you can work together to follow him. Make sure to involve everyone in your group—your small Catholic community—and have each member contribute one of the following characteristics: message, worship, or service. For example, you may propose a letter-writing campaign in which you ask a government official to help provide aid to people who are hungry. One person's role may be to write the letter, another person may pray for the success of the campaign, and the third person's job may be to deliver the letter. When your group has decided on a proposal, share it with the larger group.

A Closer Look at Confirmation

We all use words and actions to communicate with others. In a similar way, words and actions are signs of what is happening in the sacraments. The signs of Confirmation are the laying on of hands, anointing of the forehead with oil by the bishop, and the words "Be sealed with the Gift of the Holy Spirit."

The Laying on of Hands

✦ In the Old Testament the laying on of hands was a powerful sign of blessing. In the New Testament hands healed, and called down the Spirit. Read the following Scripture passages from the Bible and write what happens as a result of the laying on of hands.

Numbers 27:18–23

_____

Luke 4:40

_____

Acts of the Apostles 19:4–6

_____

❖ Anointed with Oil

Just as in baptisms and ordinations, oil is used to anoint the newly confirmed. It is called **chrism**—perfumed oil blessed by the bishop during Holy Week.

Anointing with oil is an ancient ritual to set someone apart for a special mission. In Israel priests, prophets, and kings were anointed. As we learned in Chapter 1, both *Christ* and *Messiah* come from words that mean "anointed one."

A Sacramental Seal

✦ The words of the anointing are based on the practice of stamping something for identification. In the past letters and documents were sealed with hot wax. To confirm that a message was official, a person's seal was pressed into the wax, leaving an imprint. In Confirmation God marks you as his own. You are called to receive God's mark, and you know that you are authorized to act as his disciple.

Draw here what God's seal might look like. Be as creative as you like with designs, words, and colors.

Centering on Jesus

Are you ready to live your life as a disciple of Jesus? If so, here are some ways you can do it:

Pray and celebrate the sacraments. The Eucharist and the Sacrament of Reconciliation will increase your love for Jesus.

Live the Gospel. Forming habits of Christian living and serving members of your community will help you put your faith into action.

Turn to Catholics for support and guidance. Your parents, sponsors, pastor, catechist, members of your parish, and friends preparing for Confirmation with you will help you prepare to follow Christ with them.

Study the faith. You will grow as a faithful Christian through study with this book, reflecting in your journal, and sharing your faith with your sponsor and others.

For Confirmation: Your Sponsor

A **sponsor** will be an important part of your preparation for Confirmation. At your Baptism your parents chose two sponsors for you. To emphasize the connection between Confirmation and Baptism—Confirmation seals your Baptism—you may choose one of your baptismal sponsors as your Confirmation sponsor. Or you may choose another person.

❖ Finding a Sponsor

The following paragraph shows how a classified ad requesting a Confirmation sponsor might read.

Sponsor wanted to help Confirmation candidate live his or her baptismal promises. Must be willing to share faith life with candidate and be example of Christian living, to represent the Church by supporting candidate, to pray with candidate and challenge him or her to live a Christian life, and to present candidate to minister of Confirmation. Must be a practicing Catholic, at least 16 years old, and fully initiated by Baptism, Confirmation, and the Eucharist. Preference given to candidate's baptismal sponsor. Pay: immeasurable.

This may sound like a job few people could fulfill. But you will eventually find a worthy sponsor through prayer, careful thought, and conversations with your parents or other significant adults in your life.

Your sponsor will be someone who will walk with you and offer you guidance as you prepare for Confirmation. On your day of Confirmation, he or she will literally stand behind you and confidently present you to the bishop as a person ready to be sealed with the gift of the Holy Spirit.

Read the ad with your parents and decide with them who would be a good sponsor for you. Pray to the Holy Spirit for guidance, and then discuss the responsibilities with the person you have selected.

Water
and
the Spirit

"Amen, amen, I say to you, no one can enter the kingdom of God without being born of water and Spirit."
John 3:5

Leader: We have learned about the three Sacraments of Initiation: Baptism, Confirmation, and Eucharist. Let's now listen to what Jesus tells the Pharisee Nicodemus about being born again through water and the Spirit.

Reader: A reading from the Gospel of John.
[A reader from the group reads John 3:1–5.]

The Gospel of the Lord.

All: Praise to you, Lord Jesus Christ.
[Silently reflect on God's gift of new life, which you have received.]

Reader: Now let us offer our prayers to God, who offers us new life.

That all of us who have been brought to new life in Baptism may always give thanks to God for his life in us.

All: Lord, hear our prayer.

Reader: That as we prepare to celebrate our Confirmation we may grow in understanding and living our faith.

All: Lord, hear our prayer.

Reader: That our participation in the Eucharist may nourish the new life we received in Baptism.

All: Lord, hear our prayer.

Leader: Let us conclude with the prayer Jesus taught us.

[All pray the Lord's Prayer.]

Summary

Remember

What are the Sacraments of Initiation?
The Sacraments of Initiation are Baptism, Confirmation, and the Eucharist. We are born in Baptism, strengthened in Confirmation, and nourished by the Eucharist.

What are the effects of Baptism?
Baptism is necessary for salvation, as is the Church that we enter through Baptism. It is our birth into new life in Christ. It frees us from original sin and gives us new life in Jesus. It forms a covenant between God and us, in which God promises to always be with us and to help us grow in faith. Baptism gives us sanctifying grace—new life that helps us love God and hope in him.

What does Confirmation do for us?
Confirmation seals our Baptism and deepens baptismal grace. It unites us more firmly to Christ, strengthens the Gifts of the Holy Spirit, brings us closer to the Church, and encourages us to witness to Christ in all circumstances in word and action.

What are four characteristics of the faith community formed by the Holy Spirit?
Four characteristics of Jesus' followers formed, animated, and sanctified by the Holy Spirit are community, message, worship, and service.

Words to Know
chrism	sacrament
original sin	sanctifying grace
Rite of Christian Initiation of Adults (RCIA)	sponsor

Respond

Use your journal to enter more deeply into this chapter. Begin with the prayer on page 5 of your journal. Then quietly spend time on journal pages 12–14.

Reach Out

1. Witness a Baptism at your parish. Buy or make a card that welcomes the new member to your parish community and give it to the family.

2. Ask a senior citizen in your parish to "adopt" you as you prepare for Confirmation. Visit and talk with this person about his or her faith. Ask this person to pray for you.

3. Research your parish community. Describe how it was founded and how it got its name. Describe how large the parish is, the variety of people who belong to it, and its major activities.

4. Write down your memories of your First Holy Communion. Then write a paragraph describing how your understanding and appreciation of the Eucharist has grown since then.

REVIEW

Witness, Past and Present

Read the passages from the Acts of the Apostles listed below and write the letter of the characteristic of the Church lived by these early Christians. There may be more than one.

a. Message **b.** Community

c. Worship **d.** Service

_____ 1. Acts 2:44–45 _____ 4. Acts 13:14–18

_____ 2. Acts 4:34–35 _____ 5. Acts 2:42

_____ 3. Acts 8:5–8

An Exceptional Event

Finish the sentences. If you finish them correctly the boxed letters will spell an important event involving the Holy Spirit.

1. At the Last __ __ □ __ __ __ Jesus formed a new covenant with his blood.

2. By his Death and

□ __ __ __ __ __ __ __ __ __ __ __ Jesus formed a group of people who followed his teaching and kept his commandment of love.

3. The __ __ __ __ __ __ □ __ __ are signs of the Holy Spirit's presence in our lives.

4. __ __ __ □ __ __ __ marks us as Christians.

5. Sanctifying __ __ __ __ □ helps us follow the directions of the Holy Spirit.

6. We promise to try to be like Jesus when we accept God's □ __ __ __ __ __ __ __.

7. The sacrament of

__ __ __ __ __ __ __ __ __ __ □ __ __ strengthens the gifts you received in Baptism.

8. __ __ __ □ __ __ is the oil used in Baptism and Confirmation.

9. __ □ __ __ __ __ __ __ the faith will help you grow closer to God.

What is the event? _____

Ezekiel Puzzler

Complete the crossword puzzle about the Scripture passage you read from the Book of Ezekiel.

Across

4. similar to laws or rules
6. a land not your own

Down

1. to make clean
2. pumps life to the body
3. a cleansing liquid
5. received with a new heart

3

Confirmed in Faith

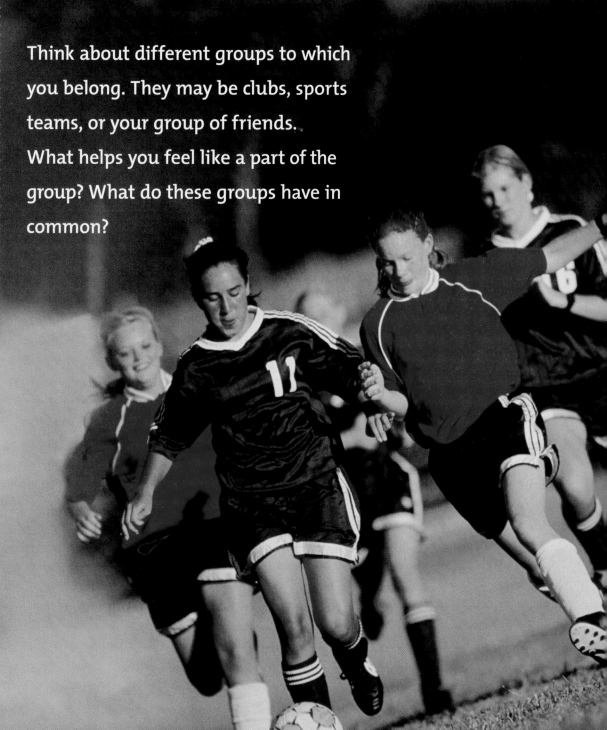

This is our faith. This is the faith of the Church. We are proud to profess it in Christ Jesus our Lord.

The Rite of Confirmation

Think about different groups to which you belong. They may be clubs, sports teams, or your group of friends. What helps you feel like a part of the group? What do these groups have in common?

Words to Take to Heart

"These then are the commandments, the statutes and decrees which the LORD, your God, has ordered that you be taught to observe in the land into which you are crossing. Hear then, Israel, and be careful to observe them, that you may grow and prosper the more, in keeping with the promise of the LORD, the God of your fathers, to give you a land flowing with milk and honey.

"Hear, O Israel! The LORD is our God, the LORD alone! Therefore, you shall love the LORD, your God, with all your heart, and with all your soul, and with all your strength. Take to heart these words which I enjoin on you today. Drill them into your children. Speak of them at home and abroad, whether you are busy or at rest."

Deuteronomy 6:1,3–7

ART Link

Marc Chagall was born in 1887 to a Jewish family in Russia. He moved to France as a young man to develop his skills as an artist. Chagall created many great works inspired by stories from the Old Testament, such as this 1956 depiction of Moses and the Tablets of the Law.

❖ Understanding Scripture

We have been talking about what helps us to feel part of a group. In the book of Deuteronomy, the last book of the **Torah**, Moses gives a number of speeches to remind the Israelites that they belong to God.

In chapter 5 of Deuteronomy, Moses restates the Ten Commandments and reminds the Israelites of all the other laws they've agreed to follow.

Moses tells the people in Deuteronomy 6:1–7 that the true way to follow God's instruction is to love God with all their heart, all their soul, and all their strength. Moses stresses that they should not only know the *words* of this instruction but that they should also take the instruction to heart, teach it to their children, and use it to guide all of their actions.

❖ Scripture and You

During this time of preparation for Confirmation, you will review important aspects of the instruction you have received. The reading from Deuteronomy should remind you that what is important in all this instruction is having a heart that loves God.

R**eflecting** *on* G**od's** W**ord**

Relax and prepare to spend some quiet time with God. Imagine that you are with all the Israelites, listening to Moses' words. God is asking you to love him with all of your heart, soul, and strength. Let his words sink in. Ask God to help you make this Confirmation preparation a time to learn more fully what it means to love him above all things.

We Believe

Just as we make a statement with the clothes we wear and the music we listen to, we make a statement by praying and living the Creed. We are stepping out into the world, telling everyone that we are Catholic and to identify us as believers.

Our faith is our personal commitment of all of our self to God. It involves the assent of our mind and will to God, who has revealed himself in words and action throughout history. We all need the support of our community to help us grow in our faith, a faith that has been handed down to us by others. During our years of instruction, we've relied on others to help us understand what the Creed means to us. In fact, the words we say in the Nicene Creed go all the way back to the fourth and fifth centuries, as *creed* comes from the Latin word *credo,* which means "I believe."

The **Trinity** is at the center of what we believe. We believe in one God who is Father, Son, and Holy Spirit. We follow Jesus because the Father calls us and the Spirit moves us. Following is a review of what we know about these three Persons in the one God.

❖ A Loving Father

Just as the Persons of the Trinity are one in what they are, they are one in what they do. God the Father is credited in a special way with the work of Creation. We believe that he is the creator of everything that exists. People wonder "Where do we come from?" and "Where are we going?" There is one answer to both of these questions: God the Father.

God the Father created us out of love and to share in his goodness. He created the entire universe by his own wisdom. But he is not an impersonal force; he is present and active in our lives. It is Jesus who teaches us to call God "Abba," Father.

God walks with us to help us achieve the goals he intended for us: eternal happiness with him, sharing his truth, goodness, and beauty.

This begins with our Baptism, which frees us from original sin. Adam and Eve's act of disobeying God resulted in original sin. This sin damaged their relationship with him and caused all humans to be born with original sin.

God our Father wished to move us from the state of original sin to the state of grace so that we, as his adopted children, could experience the intimacy of the life of the Trinity and could once again share in his holiness. So he sent his Son Jesus to be our Savior.

Revealing God in the Psalms

✦ In the Book of Psalms, favorite prayers of the Christian community, we address God with names that reveal who God is and what he means to us. Write the word used to describe God in each Scripture verse below and explain what the word tells about God.

Psalm 7:11 _____

Psalm 18:32 _____

Closer to Us

Talking to someone by phone or e-mail is nice, but visiting them in person is even better. To be closer to us, God sent his Son, Jesus, to live with us. We have been discussing the Creed, in which we state our belief that the Father sent his only Son, Jesus, to atone for our sins. Jesus is the Word of God, who became man to save us.

Jesus saved us by healing our damaged relationship with God, by revealing God's love to us, by exemplifying the holiness we should try to achieve, and by allowing us to share in his divine nature.

Divine Nature

✦ What examples of holiness from Jesus' life can you apply to your life? How might you apply them?

_____   _____

_____   _____

_____   _____

❖ Fully God, Fully Man

We are all familiar with the beautiful stories of Jesus' birth in Bethlehem. Jesus is fully God and fully man. He became man while remaining truly God. Jesus was miraculously conceived by the power of the Holy Spirit and born of the Virgin Mary.

Because she was chosen to be the Mother of God, Mary was sinless from her conception, the **Immaculate Conception.** At the end of her life, Mary's body and soul were taken to heaven in the **Assumption.**

Jesus honored Mary as his mother while he lived in Nazareth. When he was about 30 years old, he began to preach about God his Father and the Kingdom we are all called to share. For about three years he taught people how to live, and he worked miracles to show the power of the **Kingdom of God.** He invited sinners into this Kingdom.

Envious religious leaders handed Jesus over to Roman officials, claiming that he incited the crowds against Rome. The Romans crucified Jesus, he died, and he was buried. The Creed states clearly, "for our sake he was crucified." And for our sake God raised him to new life on the third day.

Jesus then appeared to his disciples and ascended to heaven to be with the Father. Our faith assures us that Jesus will come again at the end of time to judge all who have died and those still alive. He will establish God's kingdom of peace and justice forever.

On the night before he died, Jesus shared a meal with his friends. He took bread and wine and transformed them into his Body and Blood. We call this meal the Eucharist. In the Eucharist Jesus is not only present with us, but the saving events of his life, death, and Resurrection are present as well.

A Sanctifying Spirit

Sometimes when we are by ourselves we can be frustrated or lonely. Jesus made sure that we will never be alone. We just reviewed that Jesus is with us in the Eucharist. He also sent the Holy Spirit to be with us, to help us, and to defend us. The Spirit allows us to experience Jesus' saving presence. In Baptism, the first sacrament, we experience through the Holy Spirit the life that God the Father gives us in Jesus, his Son. Together the Father, the Son, and the Holy Spirit are the Trinity.

The Catholic Church

Another way Jesus made sure we would not be alone was by establishing his Church. The life of the Trinity is lived out in the Church. The Church is a community of pilgrim people on the way to the Father. These people, whom God gathers in the whole world, draw their lives from the Word and the Body of Christ and so become Christ's Body.

The Church is a visible society governed by the pope and all the other bishops, who are the successors of the apostles. They are called the **magisterium,** or teaching authority, of the Church. Guided by the Holy Spirit, they have the authority to preach the gospel and lead the Church. The bishops have the responsibility to proclaim God's message to the people.

When the pope solemnly teaches on a matter of faith and morals, the teaching is called an **infallible** teaching. This means the teaching cannot be in error.

The Church has four distinguishing marks; it is **one, holy, catholic,** and **apostolic.**

❖ One

It is one because it has been made one body in Jesus. Unity is the essence of the Church. All the baptized are members of the Church of Christ, whose fullness is found in the Roman Catholic Church. But over time there have been wounds to the Church's unity. The baptized followers of Jesus are no longer united in one Church. As Catholics we are united with Jesus in the desire to see the unity of the Church restored and should pray for and work for that end. This work toward the unity of all Christians is called **ecumenism.**

United in the Lord

✦ Make a list of things that all Christians believe. Use your list as a reminder of what Christians have in common as you pray for unity among believers in Christ.

_____

_____

_____

❖ Holy

The Church is holy because Jesus, the Church's founder, is holy. All of the Church's activities are done with the goal of making the entire world a better, holier place. The Church is always in need of purification because all its members are sinners. We are not yet the people God wants us to be; we are still on our way to becoming holy.

❖ Catholic

The Church is catholic, or open to everyone, because it has been sent by Christ to the whole human race. So even those who don't believe in Jesus are related to the Church.

The Jewish people have already given a positive response to God's call in the Old Testament. Muslims are included in God's plan of salvation because with us they adore the one, merciful God. Because it is catholic, the Church has a bond with all people through God, who created the world and everyone in it.

❖ Apostolic

The Church is apostolic because the apostles carried out Jesus' plan of establishing the Church. Today the apostles' teaching is carried out by their successors, the bishops, in union with the pope.

The mission of the Church and each of its members is the mission of Christ—to bring all creation into the Kingdom of God. To achieve this goal the Church teaches the Christian message by word and example and by serving others.

In Other Words

✦ Of one, holy, catholic, and apostolic, pick one and describe how it is important to the Church.

_____

_____

What other words can you think of that describe the Church? Write these words and explain how they describe the Church.

_____

_____

The Mother of the Church

In our families we never forget loved ones who have died. In the same way, the Church includes everyone who has died while believing in Christ and living by his example of goodness. The Communion of Saints is the Church on earth united with all those who have died and are in heaven or **purgatory.** The most esteemed member of the Communion of Saints is Mary, the Mother of God and the Church. She is our example of how the Church will be perfected in heaven.

❖ Life Everlasting

In Chapter 1 we discussed how a covenant is a promise between God and us. We can choose to keep or to break this promise. In other words, we either accept or reject the grace of God while we're alive. When we die, our time for choosing is over. We will be judged by God on the good we have done or have failed to do at this time. This is called the **Particular Judgment.**

People who die in God's grace and friendship and are perfectly purified will live forever with Christ in heaven. Those who die in friendship with God but still need to be purified of their attachment to sin experience purgatory. People who choose to completely separate themselves from God choose the state of exclusion called hell.

The **Last Judgment** will come when Christ returns in glory and pronounces the end of time as we know it. When Christ comes again, we'll know the meaning of God's plan and see how his goodness triumphs over evil. In the end God's love is stronger than death.

Growing in Faith

✦ Just as we either accept or reject God's grace, the precious gift of faith we received at Baptism can either grow or be fruitless. Like any talent—music, writing, sports—it can only grow if we practice it.

We respond to God's gifts by studying and practicing our faith. Confirmation preparation is a good time to ask questions about your faith. Your parents, your sponsor, your catechists, and your parish priest are available to discuss your questions with you. List any questions you have or ways you can learn more about your faith and grow in it.

_____

_____

For Confirmation: Learning More

How well do you understand the items under Things Every Catholic Should Know on pages 81–93? Skim through the Glossary on pages 94–98 and check the terms you understand. Look for more information about what you don't understand. Do this periodically until you know the terms well.

Our Creed

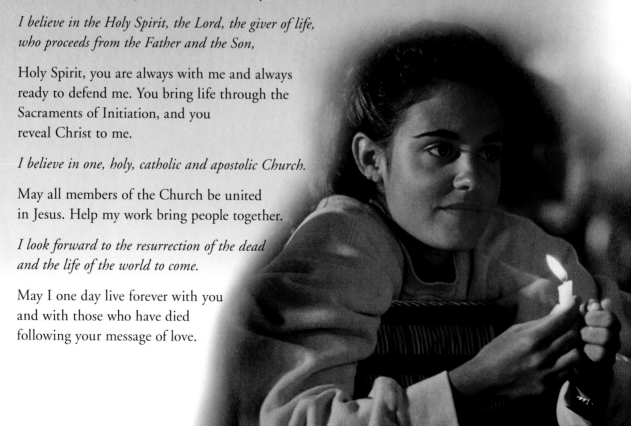

Now that we have discussed who we are as Catholics, let's reflect more deeply on the meaning of the Creed. These selected verses of the Creed, followed by passages of reflective text, will help us do so.

I believe in one God,
the Father almighty,
maker of heaven and earth,
of all things visible and invisible.

God Our Father, you created heaven and earth. You continue to care for us and for all of creation. Even though you are all-powerful, you are also my loving Father.

I believe in one Lord Jesus Christ,
the Only Begotten Son of God,
born of the Father before all ages.
God from God, Light from Light,
true God from true God,

How great you are, Lord Jesus. You are God, but you are also human like me except for sin. You are light, but you still know what it is like to be me. True God and true man, you saved me from my sins.

I believe in the Holy Spirit, the Lord, the giver of life,
who proceeds from the Father and the Son,

Holy Spirit, you are always with me and always ready to defend me. You bring life through the Sacraments of Initiation, and you reveal Christ to me.

I believe in one, holy, catholic and apostolic Church.

May all members of the Church be united in Jesus. Help my work bring people together.

I look forward to the resurrection of the dead and the life of the world to come.

May I one day live forever with you and with those who have died following your message of love.

SUMMARY

Remember

What is the statement of our faith that we pray every Sunday?

We profess the Nicene Creed at Mass every Sunday. It contains the main truths of the Catholic faith.

What is at the center of our faith?

The Trinity is at the center of our faith. We believe in one God, who is Father, Son, and Holy Spirit.

How did God move us from the state of sin to the state of grace?

God sent his Son, Jesus, to be our Savior, to save us from our sins. Jesus fixes our damaged relationship with God, reveals God's love to us, and allows us to share in his divine nature.

What are the four distinguishing marks of the Church?

The Church is one, holy, catholic, and apostolic.

What is the Communion of Saints?

The Communion of Saints is the Church on earth united with all those who have died and are in heaven or purgatory. Mary, the Mother of God and the Church, is the most esteemed member of the Communion of Saints.

When will we fully understand the meaning of God's plan?

We will understand God's plan at the Last Judgment, when Christ returns in glory and pronounces the end of time as we know it.

Words to Know

apostolic	Assumption
catholic	creation
ecumenism	holy
Immaculate Conception	infallible
Kingdom of God	Last Judgment
magisterium	Nicene Creed
one	purgatory
Particular Judgment	Trinity
Torah	

Respond

Use your journal to enter more deeply into this chapter. Begin with the prayer on page 5 of your journal. Then quietly spend time on journal pages 18–20.

Reach Out

1. Memorize the Act of Faith on the inside back cover of your book by praying it often.

2. List ways you can act so that the people who meet you will know you are Catholic.

3. Start a discussion on some aspect of what we believe as Catholics with a friend or family member.

REVIEW

Make It True

Cross out the word(s) or letter(s) that makes each sentence false. Then make each sentence true by writing the correct word(s) above the crossed out word(s).

1. Catholics believe in three Gods.

2. *Creed* comes from the Latin word *credo,* which means "I am with you."

3. Jesus worked miracles to show the power of God's creation.

4. The Catholic Church is a community of people from all over the United States.

5. The goal of unity for all Christians is called *ecclesiasticism.*

6. The Church is holy because Peter, the Church's founder, is holy.

7. The Church teaches the Christian message by word only.

8. The Church is *catholic,* or open only to those who are born into the faith.

9. Mary is equal to all the other members of the Communion of Saints.

10. People who die in God's grace and friendship will live forever with Christ in purgatory.

Trios of Truth

Complete each list of three.

three Persons of the Trinity

_____

_____

_____

three states of being that humans can reach after dying

_____

_____

_____

three of the four distinguishing marks of the Church

_____

_____

Catholic or Not?

Write a *C* before the beliefs that are held by Catholics.

___ **1.** Jesus is true God and similar to true man.

___ **2.** God the Father is credited in a special way with the work of creation.

___ **3.** Adam and Eve's offense resulted in original sin.

___ **4.** Mary was sinless from her conception.

___ **5.** Jesus preached God's word but did not do good works.

___ **6.** After his Resurrection, Jesus never appeared to his disciples.

___ **7.** For about three years, Jesus preached about God his Father and the Kingdom we are called to share.

___ **8.** The Church is called the Body of Christ.

Confirmed in Love

How many choices do you make each day? How often do you make a really important choice? Where do you turn for help in making those important choices?

Pour out, we pray, the gifts of the Holy Spirit across the face of the earth and, with the divine grace that was at work when the Gospel was first proclaimed, fill now once more the hearts of believers.

Collect prayer, Pentecost

The Beatitudes

Blessed are the poor in spirit,
  for theirs is the kingdom of
  heaven.

Blessed are they who mourn,
  for they will be comforted.

Blessed are the meek,
  for they will inherit the land.

Blessed are they who hunger
  and thirst for righteousness,
  for they will be satisfied.

Blessed are the merciful,
  for they will be shown mercy.

Blessed are the clean of heart,
  for they will see God.

Blessed are the peacemakers,
  for they will be called children of
  God.

Blessed are they who are
  persecuted for the sake of
  righteousness,
  for theirs is the kingdom of heaven.

Blessed are you when they insult you
and persecute you and utter every
kind of evil against you [falsely]
because of me. Rejoice and be
glad, for your reward will be great
in heaven. Thus they persecuted the
prophets who were before you.
Matthew 5:3–12.

❖ Understanding Scripture

We've been talking about needing help when making difficult choices. Jesus tells us we can find that help in the **Beatitudes** and the **Ten Commandments.** The Beatitudes begin the Sermon on the Mount, the first of five long teaching sections in the Gospel. In this sermon Jesus gives his new interpretation to many of the laws given by Moses in the five books of the Torah. So it is fitting that Jesus calls his followers to a new way of living that moves beyond the core of the law given by Moses, the Ten Commandments.

With the Beatitudes, Jesus is offering us a new way of life. If we live according to the Beatitudes, we can begin to experience the Kingdom of God.

❖ Scripture and You

As we know from experience, making moral decisions is never easy. The Ten Commandments give us directions—"Keep the Lord's day holy," "Do not kill," "Do not steal," and others. But they are not always easy to follow. The Beatitudes are a bit different. They are not so much a description of what we should do, but rather they are examples of whom we should be, and not just as individuals but as members of a community for whom the Kingdom of God is both a promise and a present reality.

God wants us to be happy, and following the Beatitudes will help us find happiness. God made us with the desire for happiness so that we would be drawn to him, the one who can make us completely happy.

Each beatitude begins with the Greek word *makarios,* which can be translated "happy." But because they are about the happiness that comes from drawing nearer to the Kingdom of God, "blessed" is the best translation. The happiness we are called to can't be found in riches, fame, or any human achievement; it can only come from trusting God.

The Ten Commandments and the Sermon on the Mount describe the path that leads to true happiness. Sustained by the Holy Spirit we walk that path, step by step, in our everyday actions.

Reflecting *on* **God's Word**

Relax your body and calm your mind. Think about times you find it difficult to do what you know you should. Think about Jesus' words of blessing to you in the Beatitudes. Ask him for help in your difficult times.

Called to Be Free

We can only be truly happy if we are free, or responsible for our own actions. So God created us to be free. It is within our power to choose to do what is good or not to do it. Our freedom means we are responsible for our actions. The more we choose to do what is good, the freer we become. But choosing to be happy, choosing to be free, is not always easy. The right choice is not always clear.

Any choice you make to do good needs to meet three requirements. First, what you want to do must be good. Helping a friend, cleaning up around the yard, visiting a sick neighbor—these are all good actions. Second, your intention must be good as well. Doing a chore for a neighbor to avoid baby-sitting your sister is not an example of choosing good. When the reason you want to do something is not good, even a kind act is not the right decision.

Finally, the circumstances of the choice must be considered. An example of this would be if you promised your parents that you would come straight home after school, but on the way home your friend twisted his ankle. You walked with him to make sure he got home safely, and you were late arriving at your home as a result. The circumstances made your decision more difficult. You were called to make a much more mature decision, taking into account the needs of your neighbor. It is not always easy to choose according to your conscience, but that is what growing as a Christian is about.

❖ Conscience: Where We Hear God Speak

How do we know what is a good choice? How do we know our intentions are good? Deep within us is a voice that helps us to know right from wrong and to act on that knowledge. When we take time to put aside distractions and look inside ourselves, we find our **conscience.** Because we are made in the image of God, the highest good, and drawn to him, our conscience naturally directs us toward choosing good and avoiding evil.

But because of original sin we can be tempted to go against our conscience. The formation of our conscience is a life-long task. It begins in our family and continues through following the teaching of the Church, the friendships we build, and the choices we make. But it is our responsibility to continue to form our conscience as we grow. As we will see in the next chapter, the virtues and Gifts of the Spirit will help us do this.

Right and Wrong

✦ For each bad decision, write a good choice that could be made instead.

Erica leaves her grandmother at the store when she realizes she is running late for soccer practice.

_____

_____

Dominic forgets to do his homework, so he tells the teacher that his little brother tore it up.

_____

Actions Speak Louder Than Words

Does the way you behave let people know you are a Catholic? Read the situations and consider whether you ever act in these ways.

- Let someone else be the center of attention.
- Go out of your way to make a new person feel comfortable and welcomed.
- Volunteer even when none of your friends do.
- Avoid passing on rumors.
- Sacrifice your free time to visit someone who is sick.
- Admit when you have done something wrong and apologize.

You know what influence a rock musician, a movie star, or a sports hero can have on your life. You adopt their style of clothing, their likes and dislikes, and maybe even copy their walk, gestures, or expressions. Jesus Christ is our greatest role model and guide for our lives. He instructed us to keep the Ten Commandments. When asked what was the greatest commandment he responded:

"You shall love the Lord your God with all your heart, with all your soul, with all your mind, and with all your strength." And he added, "The second is this: You shall love your neighbor as yourself." *Mark 12:30–31*

At another time he said: "I give you a new commandment: love one another. As I have loved you, so you also should love one another." *John 13:34*

Loving God and loving our neighbors is what the Ten Commandments are all about. Review the Ten Commandments in the Things Every Catholic Should Know section in the back of your book. Choose one commandment and think of an example of one way that keeping it shows love of God or neighbor.

Christian Love

Loving like Jesus means making room in our hearts for all people—our families, our friends, our parish community, our brothers and sisters in other countries, even people we don't especially like. We can do this by showing the warmth, love, and acceptance of Jesus Christ to the poor, the sick, strangers, even those who have hurt us. Jesus appreciated the response of love he found in people. He praised positive attitudes, generosity, and service.

✦ Can you recognize love? Read the Gospel verses below. Underline the responses of love that people gave.

1. Mary, the sister of Martha (Luke 10:38–42)
   kindness   listening   service

2. Martha (Luke 10:38–42)
   serving   healing   listening

3. The Samaritan leper (Luke 17:11–19)
   generosity   preaching   expressing thanks

4. The centurion (Luke 7:1–10)
   teaching   faith   patience

5. Andrew (John 1:40–42)
   joy   singing   leading a friend to Jesus

6. Joseph of Arimathea (Matthew 27:57–60)
   preaching   patience   sharing possessions

7. The women who followed Jesus (Luke 8:1–3)
   hospitality   patience   trust

8. Zacchaeus, the tax collector (Luke 19:1–10)
   listening   repentance   mercy

9. The good Samaritan (Luke 10:29–37)
   mercy   faith   humility

10. The man who was blind and begging by the roadside (Luke 18:35–43)
    generosity   teaching   faith

What response of love does Jesus ask from Peter? (Matthew 18:1–22)

_____

What response of love have you witnessed lately?

_____

_____

_____

_____

_____

Christian Service

At Baptism we received the grace that enables us to love and serve others without counting the cost, to see Christ in them, and to avoid hurting them. Grace makes us eager to reach out to others with concern. It leads us to use our gifts and talents to meet their needs. Confirmation helps our love grow stronger.

We show we have loving hearts when we perform works of mercy. As members of the Christian community, we are actively concerned about those who do not have enough clothing, food, or a good home. We meet their physical needs through the **corporal works of mercy.** These works include feeding the hungry, sheltering the homeless, clothing the naked, visiting the sick and imprisoned, burying the dead, and giving alms to the poor.

We also want to help those who are feeling hurt, discouraged, sick, or confused. We meet the emotional and spiritual needs of people through the **spiritual works of mercy.** These works are instructing, advising, consoling, comforting, forgiving, and bearing wrongs patiently. The Spirit helps us know what to do to come to the aid of our neighbor.

Works of Mercy

✦ Write an example of Jesus performing a corporal work of mercy, and write the Bible passage where it is described.

_____

_____

Write an example of Jesus performing a spiritual work of mercy, and write the Bible passage where it is described.

_____

_____

❖ Justice

A way to love and serve others—through the spiritual or corporal works of mercy—is to protect their basic rights. Every person in the world has the right to food, clothing, shelter, and fair wages. Every person has the right to life and to freedom. Sometimes we work for justice by giving people what they need. But sometimes justice means speaking up for people, teaching them, and standing up for them. Justice is a matter of love.

Working for Justice

✦ Think about what you have seen on TV or read about in the newspaper. Who is in need of justice today? Write what you can do to help.

_____

_____

❖ *Service*

Your attitudes toward service can teach people how to have a heart for others. Think about it. Is your attitude toward service positive? Do you look for ways to serve others? Do you consider it a privilege to serve? Followers of Jesus who believe in their hearts that he loves them will show the same love to others.

When we reach out to others in service with the joy and strength of the Holy Spirit, we find we are the ones who really receive. We receive Christ, who lives in the people we serve.

Nominations for Greatness

✦ The secret of greatness is given in Mark 10:42–44. What does Jesus say it is?

_____

_____

A great person has a heart for others. Whom would you nominate for the kind of greatness Jesus describes?

_____

_____

For Confirmation: Practicing Christian Service

As Christians, we are called to serve others. Think about how you can volunteer your time and talent for the good of the community. Keep a record of the service you do during your time of preparation for Confirmation. Write about it in your journal regularly. After you have reached out to others in Christian service, reflect on your experience. You might complete the following statements on pages 27–29 of your journal:

I tried to show Christian love and service by . . .

I chose to do this because . . .

By doing this service, I learned that Christian service means . . .

Doing this service helped me . . .

Two important events that happened to me while doing this project were . . .

These people taught me . . .

This experience will help me later in life because it taught me . . .

I can follow up on this experience by . . .

Act of Love

Quietly pray this prayer. Then spend time reflecting on the thoughts that follow.

O my God, I love you above all things,

with my whole heart and soul,

because you are all-good and worthy of all my love.

I love my neighbor as myself for the love of you.

I forgive all who have injured me,

and I ask pardon of all whom I have injured.

Amen.

Choosing to do good is choosing to love. In preparing for Confirmation you are considering ways you express your love of God and your neighbor, your willingness to forgive others, and your desire to be forgiven. Silently thank God for filling you with these acts of love. Ask him to strengthen your love of him and others and to help you forgive those who have offended you. Talk to God about whatever is in your heart.

Summary

Remember

What are the Beatitudes?
The Beatitudes are Jesus' guidelines for Christian living. Each one includes an attitude and the promise of happiness in God's kingdom.

What is your conscience?
Conscience is that deepest part of yourself that directs you toward choosing good and avoiding evil.

What is Jesus' new commandment?
"I give you a new commandment: love one another. As I have loved you, so you also should love one another."
John 13:34

Words to Know
Beatitudes

corporal works of mercy

conscience

spiritual works of mercy

Ten Commandments

Respond

Use your journal to enter more deeply into this chapter. Begin with the prayer on page 5 of your journal. Then quietly spend time on journal pages 24–26.

Reach Out

1. Neatly letter the Beatitudes on white drawing paper. Decorate around them. Paste the sheet in your journal or put it where you will see it at home.

2. Read a biography of a Christian known for service.

3. Begin your Christian service at home.

4. Do what you are told without complaining.

5. Cooperate with family projects.

6. Share with your brothers and sisters.

7. Volunteer to do more than you have to when helping around the house.

8. Pray for your family.

Evaluate how often you reach out in love. For each response of love, mentally rate yourself 1 (not very often), 2 (sometimes), or 3 (often). Think about how you can improve where you are weakest.

_____ Listen

_____ Be an example of a good Catholic for others

_____ Serve

_____ Forgive

_____ Express thanks

_____ Share with others

_____ Pray

_____ Welcome others

Review

Service Word Search

Circle the following words in the word search.

Beatitudes   conscience   corporal

kingdom   service   spiritual

```
F  R  W  X  S  L  C  E  M  E
O  W  C  G  E  C  O  C  R  E
L  C  M  O  D  G  N  I  K  U
B  O  N  S  U  I  S  V  R  Y
E  R  P  N  T  U  C  R  A  J
V  P  O  Y  I  P  I  E  O  M
I  O  Y  S  T  B  E  S  L  Q
P  R  C  V  A  O  N  L  U  X
K  A  J  B  E  W  C  W  C  M
X  L  F  W  B  A  E  C  L  B
I  S  P  I  R  I  T  U  A  L
```

Make It True

Write *T* for *true* and *F* for *false*. Make each false statement true.

___ **1.** The Beatitudes begin the Sermon on the Mount.

_____

___ **2.** The core of the law, the Ten Commandments, was given by God to Moses.

_____

___ **3.** It was easy for Jesus' community to follow the Beatitudes.

_____

___ **4.** Your intention must be good in order to make a good choice.

_____

___ **5.** The Beatitudes replace the Ten Commandments.

_____

___ **6.** Your conscience naturally directs you toward evil.

_____

Confirmation Crossword

Across

1. called children of God

4. Jesus appreciated this in people.

5. directs us toward good

6. We are called to provide it.

Down

2. Moses gave us these.

3. Our conscience helps us make good ones.

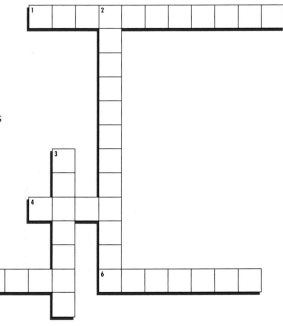

Confirmed in Holiness

Send your Holy Spirit upon them to be their Helper and Guide. Give them the spirit of wisdom and understanding, the spirit of right judgment and courage, the spirit of knowledge and reverence. Fill them with the spirit of wonder and awe in your presence.

The Rite of Confirmation

What are some of your talents? What are some things you do to improve them? Name some of the ways you are trying to put your talents to good use.

Led by the Spirit

For those who are led by the Spirit of God are children of God. For you did not receive a spirit of slavery to fall back into fear, but you received a spirit of adoption, through which we cry, "Abba, Father!" The Spirit itself bears witness with our spirit that we are children of God....In the same way, the Spirit too comes to the aid of our weakness; for we do not know how to pray as we ought, but the Spirit itself intercedes with inexpressible groanings. And the one who searches hearts knows what is the intention of the Spirit, because it intercedes for the holy ones according to God's will.

We know that all things work for good for those who love God, who are called according to his purpose.

Romans 8:14–16,26–28

In this retablo, a special Mexican art form, the Father is shown with a sun, the Son with a lamb, and the Holy Spirit with a dove. The Spirit calls us into this Trinity with Jesus and leads us to call God "Abba," "Father."

❖ Understanding Scripture

Trying to put your talents to use is hard work. But Paul's words to the Christians in Rome encourage us. Paul is reminding them that through Jesus' death and the Spirit they received, they have really become God's children. Gentiles as well as Jews can now call God *Abba,* or *Father.* The people God formed through Abraham now include the Gentiles as well. The letter to the Romans discusses how the effects of Adam's sin have been reversed in Jesus, the new Adam. It also explains how the sufferings the Gentiles endure are overcome by the hope that they have been given through the "spirit of adoption."

❖ Scripture and You

All of us excel in certain areas and struggle in others. Because we are adopted children of God, we are able to use our talents in spite of our natural weaknesses. When prayer is difficult for us, the Spirit intercedes, helping us to be good, even holy. In this chapter we will look more closely at the gifts the Holy Spirit gives to help us.

Reflecting *on* **God's Word**

As you quiet yourself for prayer, be aware of your breath as you slowly breathe in and out. Invite the Holy Spirit to help you with anything in your life with which you may be struggling. Conclude by giving thanks for the Spirit's guidance.

The Theological Virtues

Aaron began taking piano lessons when he was six. Taking time every day was not easy, and he had many disagreements with his parents about whether he had practiced enough. He wanted to be out playing with his friends and enjoying his free time. But there was something he really enjoyed about making music, so he stuck with it. Now at fourteen, he's glad he continued playing the piano. There are still times he would rather do anything but practice, but he realizes now that he doesn't have to think too much about the physical part of playing. He can let the skills he has developed lead him and use his heart to create beautiful music.

As children of God, we receive through the Spirit the **theological virtues** of **faith, hope,** and **charity.** These virtues have their source in God, are infused in us by him, and as we grow in using them, we are drawn more deeply into the mystery of God. That is why they are called "theological."

Practicing these **virtues** strengthens us over time and helps us make good decisions and give the best of ourselves.

❖ Faith

Faith, God's gift to you, is the ability to believe in God and give your life to him. It makes you able to trust God completely and to accept all that God has revealed and teaches through the Catholic Church.

❖ Hope

Hope is closely related to faith. It is the desire for all of the good things God has planned for you. Hope gives you confidence that God will always be with you and that you will live with God forever in heaven.

❖ Charity

Charity leads you to love God above all things and your neighbor as yourself. This love involves more than just feelings; it is the way you think about God and act toward him. Charity brings all the virtues together in perfect harmony. "So faith, hope, love remain," Saint Paul writes in 1 Corinthians 13:13, "but the greatest of these is love."

As you practice the virtues of faith, hope, and charity and grow in your relationship with God, your ability to practice the **cardinal virtues** also grows.

The Cardinal Virtues

The virtues you acquire by human effort are called cardinal virtues. *Cardinal* comes from the Latin *cardo,* which means "hinge." All of your moral strengths depend on these virtues. They are **prudence, justice, fortitude,** and **temperance.** These human virtues are rooted in the theological virtues that are given to you by God to help you act as his child.

❖ Prudence

Prudence helps you to decide what is good and then to choose to do it. It leads you to stop and think before you act.

❖ Justice

Justice leads you to respect the rights of others and to give them what is rightfully theirs. The just person considers the needs of others and always tries to be fair.

❖ Fortitude

Fortitude gives you the courage to do what is right even when it is very difficult. It provides you the strength to resist the temptations you face and, even when it is difficult, to do what you know is right.

❖ Temperance

Temperance helps you balance what you want with what you need. It helps you moderate your desire for enjoyment and builds self-control.

Like playing the piano, being a good friend, playing sports, or anything else worthwhile, these virtues take time and effort to develop. But through practice they can become a natural part of your life. With God's help the cardinal virtues build character and make it easier to do what is right. These virtues will help you to achieve whatever goals you have.

How Virtues Help Us

✦ Describe a situation in which you displayed one of the virtues. Which virtue did you display, and how did it help you?

_____

_____

_____

_____

Unwrapping the Gifts of the Spirit

The cardinal and theological virtues are strengths that can improve your life if you practice them. The **Gifts of the Holy Spirit,** which you received at Baptism, help you to live a life of virtue. These gifts are strengthened in Confirmation. They help you keep your friendship with God strong and guide you in critical situations when you find it hard to cope with problems or to make decisions. They help you respond to God fully and lovingly.

Four gifts help you to know God's will. The other three help you to do his will.

Know God's Will	Do God's Will
wisdom	courage
understanding	reverence
right judgment	wonder and awe
knowledge	

Read about each gift of the Spirit below. The questions will help you reflect on how he is already at work in your life.

❖ Wisdom

Just as piano players' music becomes more complicated the longer they play, life becomes more complex the older you get. Everywhere you turn, people are telling you how to act, what to wear, what to believe, whom your friends should be, and what music to listen to. How do you know what is best for you?

Wisdom enables you to see life from God's point of view and to recognize the real value of persons, events, and things. Wisdom keeps you from foolishly judging only by appearances. It makes you mature in the way you think and act. Wisdom leads you to work toward being confirmed not because your parents expect it, or because everyone your age is doing it, but because you see its value and desire it.

❖ Understanding

When you were younger you learned that there were things you should and should not do. You learned rules and followed them because you trusted people who made them, such as your parents. You also didn't want to be punished for disobeying the rules, but you didn't always understand why they were made. The same might be true with your faith. So how will you be able to really understand what it means to be Catholic?

Understanding grows through prayer and the reading of Scripture. It gives you insight into the truths of the faith and being a follower of Jesus, and it helps you make right choices in your relationships with God and others.

❖ Right Judgment

Have you ever agonized over a difficult decision? Did it make you feel confused, hurt, and alone? How did you know what was the right thing to do?

The gift of **right judgment,** or counsel, helps you seek advice and be open to the advice of others. Using this gift, you seek direction in the Sacrament of Penance, and you ask advice from parents or friends. Right judgment also helps you give advice. With right judgment, you are able to help others with their problems. You speak up and encourage them to do the right thing.

Today, through the gift of right judgment, you are determining what being confirmed means in your life. You turn to your parents, parish priest, catechists, and others for help in taking this next step in your spiritual journey.

❖ Knowledge

Having an awareness of God's plan will help you to live a meaningful life. Knowing Jesus' teachings and bringing them to heart will help you to be a good Christian. How can you become open to what God has to teach you about life?

The gift of **knowledge** helps you know what God asks of you and how you should respond. You come to know God. You come to know who you are and the real value of things through the experiences of your life. This gift also helps you recognize temptations for what they are and turn to God for help.

The gift of knowledge is at work in you as you think about your experience of living a Christian life. What you know of Jesus and his example and what you know of the Church—its worship, its beliefs, its directives to serve those in need—will help you commit yourself to Christ and the Church as a confirmed Christian.

❖ Courage

It is one thing to know the right thing to do. It is something else to be able to do it. You face a lot of pressure about using drugs and alcohol. Movies and songs tell you that sex is just about feeling good. It's not always cool to speak out about injustices you see around you. How can you find the strength to live by the principles and values of Jesus?

The gift of **courage,** or fortitude, enables you to stand up for your beliefs and to live as a follower of Jesus. With this gift you have the inner strength to do what is right in the face of difficulties and to endure suffering with faith. Courage helps you to undertake challenging tasks in the service of your faith. But it also takes courage to be faithful to ordinary duties. It takes strength to live a good Christian life even when no one praises you or notices your effort.

Right now you are deciding to reflect on your faith seriously. It is difficult to try to change your habits and follow Jesus more completely. It's a challenge to pray more, to participate in the Eucharist more intentionally, to serve others.

❖ Reverence

It is not uncommon to see people showing
little respect for others, for the environment, even for
themselves. They destroy things that God has given
us to enjoy. This wouldn't happen if people had a sense of
God's presence in others and in the world. How can you be
more aware of God's presence in your life and in others?

Reverence, or piety, is a gift that helps you love and worship
God. It calls you to be faithful in your relationships with
God and others. Reverence also helps you to be respectful and
generous to others.

In the Sacrament of Confirmation, reverence helps you
strengthen your relationship with God and increase your love
for others and the world.

❖ Wonder and Awe

Out of respect, Moses removed his sandals when God spoke to him from the burning
bush. Many Jews today never even dare to pronounce the name of God. We can
learn from their examples by honoring God, who is awesome and who loves us.

The gift of **wonder and awe,** sometimes called fear of the Lord, helps you recognize
the greatness of God and your dependence on him. It leads you to marvel at God's
incredible love for you.

Wonder and awe is increasing your desire to draw closer to God by confirming the
great gift you received in Baptism. Awe will inspire you to celebrate the Eucharist
and the Sacrament of Penance, when you ask forgiveness for the times you failed
to respond to God's great love.

Your Favorite Gift

✦ Think of someone you know who exemplifies at least one of the Gifts of the Spirit.
With which gift do you most identify this person? How does this gift lead the person
to live his or her life?

_____

_____

_____

_____

For Confirmation: Letter Requesting the Sacrament

Requesting the Sacrament of Confirmation from your bishop or pastor is a
way to let him know that you are serious in your desire for the sacrament.
You may wish to mention in the letter one or two ways you are trying to
take your faith more seriously and some ways you have given service.

My Lord and Guardian

We know that God has blessed us with many gifts to help us live the life he intended for us. Let us pray this psalm and reflect on these wonderful gifts from the Lord.

Psalm 121

Group A *I raise my eyes toward the mountains.*
From where will my help come?
My help comes from the LORD,
the maker of heaven and earth.

Group B *God will not allow your foot to slip;*
your guardian does not sleep.
Truly, the guardian of Israel
never slumbers nor sleeps.

Group A *The LORD is your guardian;*
the LORD is your shade
at your right hand.
By day the sun cannot harm you,
nor the moon by night.

Group B *The LORD will guard you from all evil,*
will always guard your life.
The LORD will guard your coming and going
both now and forever.

Group A *Glory be to the Father, and to the Son, and to the Holy Spirit,*

Group B *As it was in the beginning, is now, and ever shall be, world without end.*

All *Amen.*

Silently spend some time talking and listening to God from your heart. Ask him whatever you would like and listen for his response.

Summary

Remember

What are the Gifts of the Spirit?

The Gifts of the Spirit are powers given to us at Baptism and strengthened at Confirmation. They help us live virtuous lives, persevere in our friendship with God, and guide us in our decisions and conduct so we become more like Jesus.

How is the greatest virtue—charity, or love—described in Scripture?

Love is patient, love is kind. It is not jealous, [love] is not pompous, it is not inflated, it is not rude, it does not seek its own interests, it is not quick-tempered, it does not brood over injury, it does not rejoice over wrongdoing but rejoices with the truth. It bears all things, believes all things, hopes all things, endures all things.
I Corinthians 13:4–7

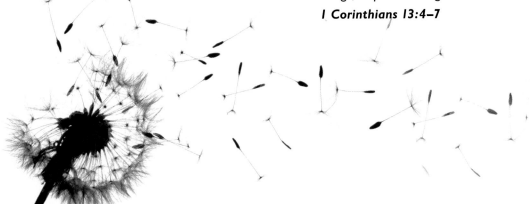

Respond

Use your journal to enter more deeply into this chapter. Begin with the prayer on page 5 in your journal. Then quietly spend time on journal pages 30–32.

Words to Know

cardinal virtues	prudence
charity	reverence
courage	right judgment
faith	temperance
fortitude	theological virtues
Gifts of the Holy Spirit	understanding
hope	virtues
justice	wisdom
knowledge	wonder and awe

Reach Out

1. You and your friends preparing for Confirmation might make banners depicting the seven Gifts of the Spirit to display in a suitable place at the time of your Confirmation.

2. Titus was a young bishop and a friend of Saint Paul. Read Titus 3:1–2. What signs of the Spirit is Titus urged to show? Explain in a paragraph how these can help you show loving service.

3. Write your sponsor a note telling about the Gifts of the Spirit you see in his or her life.

REVIEW

Gifts from God

In the box write the Gift of the Spirit that goes with each definition.

enables you to love the things of God and to see things from his point of view

[   ]

helps you to know the value of things through your life experiences

[   ]

enables you to love and respect God and others

[   ]

gives you strength to stand up for your beliefs

[   ]

gives you insights into the truths of the faith

[   ]

allows you to recognize God's greatness

[   ]

helps you seek advice and be open to the advice of others

[   ]

A Gallery of Gifts and Virtues

Match each gift or virtue with the sentence that describes a person displaying it.

a. fortitude	**h.** hope
b. faith	**i.** prudence
c. charity	**j.** reverence
d. right judgment	**k.** temperance
e. justice	**l.** knowledge
f. wonder and awe	**m.** courage
g. wisdom	**n.** understanding

—— **1.** considers others' needs and values fairness

—— **2.** makes right choices in relationships with God and others

—— **3.** recognizes God's greatness and our dependence on him

—— **4.** resists temptation and does what's right even when it's difficult

—— **5.** knows the meaning of Jesus' teachings

—— **6.** stops and thinks before acting

—— **7.** aware of the presence of God in others

—— **8.** trusts God completely and believes all he has revealed through the Church

—— **9.** stands up for beliefs and lives as a follower of God

—— **10.** loves God and neighbor because of God's love for us

—— **11.** seeks good advice and receives it from others

—— **12.** sees life from God's point of view

—— **13.** exhibits self-control and limits desire for enjoyment

—— **14.** has confidence that God will be with us forever

Confirmed *in the* Church

Grant that we, who are nourished by the Body and Blood of your Son and filled with his Holy Spirit, may become one body, one spirit in Christ.

Eucharistic Prayer III

What makes a celebration special for you? Is it the people, the music, the food? What can you do to help everyone feel included?

Put On Love

Put on then, as God's chosen ones, holy and beloved, heartfelt compassion, kindness, humility, gentleness, and patience, bearing with one another and forgiving one another, if one has a grievance against another; as the Lord has forgiven you, so must you also do. And over all these put on love, that is, the bond of perfection. And let the peace of Christ control your hearts, the peace into which you were also called in one body. And be thankful. Let the word of Christ dwell in you richly, as in all wisdom you teach and admonish one another, singing psalms, hymns, and spiritual songs with gratitude in your hearts to God. And whatever you do, in word or in deed, do everything in the name of the Lord Jesus, giving thanks to God the Father through him.

Colossians 3:12–17

ART Link

Christ in Majesty is from an 11th-century illuminated manuscript. It was painted in a hand-written book using finely ground pigment mixed with egg white, fig sap, or a thin glue. Jesus is presiding over heaven and earth as a reminder that we should do everything in his name and give thanks to God through him.

❖ Understanding Scripture

Like a father who is concerned about his child's welfare, God the Father cares deeply about our well-being. So he sent his Son Jesus to save us. The Letter to the Colossians describes many of the good things God the Father has done for us through Jesus.

In this section the virtuous life, which you reviewed in the last chapter, is described once again as reaching its perfection in love. You are putting on the virtuous life. Now let the peace of Christ fill you as you give thanks to God the Father through Jesus. In him we have become members of a community so united that it is "one body." In this community we are to live in peace and thanksgiving as we do everything in the name of the Lord Jesus.

❖ Scripture and You

Each morning as you put on your clothes, do you ever think about also putting on kindness or gentleness or patience? That's not as easy as it sounds, but fortunately, you don't have to try to do it alone. Luckily it is not just up to you. God the Father and his Son Jesus sent the Holy Spirit to help you to live in kindness. The peace of Christ and the word of Christ, which dwell in you, also support you in living peacefully.

In the Church we have sacraments, beginning with Baptism, which help us wear love like our favorite clothes. In the Sacrament of Penance our sins are forgiven; we find pardon and peace. In the Eucharist we share in the very life of Jesus. These two sacraments help us to accept and forgive one another as we live lives of peace and thanksgiving.

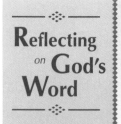

Reflecting *on* **God's Word**

Take some time to center yourself, quietly breathing in and out. Silently reflect on the words compassion, kindness, humility, gentleness, and patience. Think about which of these qualities you would like God to help you strengthen. Ask for his help now.

Many, Yet One

A young woman serving as a missionary in New Guinea brings Holy Communion to a dying mother. Mexican children sing and clap as they process to church for the feast-day Mass of the patron of their town, the Virgin of San Juan de los Lagos. Pope John Paul II canonizes 103 Korean martyrs at a majestic solemn Mass in Rome. A small group of Chinese Catholics gather for Mass in an apartment just outside Beijing.

What makes all of these people one? How are we united with the Church in New Guinea, Mexico, Korea, and China? The Church in this world is the sacrament of salvation for all. The Church is the instrument that makes the communion between God and people possible. When we come together to celebrate the Eucharist, we are united with the Church throughout the world and with all the angels and saints as well. We are one through Jesus, the bread of life. In the Eucharist our bonds with the worldwide Church are strengthened. We belong not only to our parish community but also to the universal Church as well.

When we are with our friends, we feel we belong. Every moment is important. We listen intently to what they have to say. We participate in the conversation excitedly. Time goes by quickly, and we make plans to get together again.

Because of our Baptism, we belong to the Body of Christ, the Church, and all the members are our friends in Christ. When we participate in the Eucharist, we strengthen our friendships with Jesus, whose love for us is so great. We worship God, offer together the sacrifice of Calvary, and enter into the **Paschal Mystery** of Jesus' life, death, and Resurrection. Our life as Catholics comes from the Eucharist and leads to the Eucharist. This sacrament helps us to love and serve as Jesus did. It does this through the work of the Spirit.

❖ Jesus Alive!

The Spirit makes Jesus available to the world. When Mary said yes to God, it was through the Spirit that Jesus was conceived in her. When the Spirit descended on the disciples at Pentecost, they proclaimed that Jesus was alive in the world. When the Spirit came to you in Baptism, Christ became alive in you. During the Mass the Spirit speaks through the Scriptures. Then, in the Eucharistic prayer, the priest prays that through the power of the Holy Spirit, Jesus Christ becomes present under the appearance of bread and wine. And Jesus is with us.

The Holy Spirit is the Spirit of Jesus bringing you closer to himself. He makes you one with Jesus in the Mass, when you offer to the Father your joys, sorrows, successes, and failures. The Spirit works in the community that is gathered to receive the Eucharist, and unites all members of this community in faith and love.

✦ Work in groups to think of ways the Eucharist strengthens relationships in your parish. Record your thoughts, and then share them with the larger group.

_____

_____

_____

Liturgy of the Word

The Mass has two main parts: the **Liturgy of the Word** and the **Liturgy of the Eucharist.** Both God's Word and Christ's Body and Blood unite us and nourish us as people of God.

In the Liturgy of the Word, you are united with other members of God's family. Just as you hear family members' stories when you celebrate with loved ones, so do you hear God's stories when you gather for the Liturgy of the Word at Mass.

The Power of God's Word

✦ When you think deeply about God's Word, it makes a difference in your life. Reflect on the following readings often used in the Confirmation liturgy. Think about how they speak of unity in believing, living, and proclaiming God's message.

First Reading: Acts 1:8
"You will receive power when the holy Spirit comes upon you, and you will be my witnesses."
Name two ways members of your parish are united as witnesses to Jesus.

_____

_____

Gospel Reading: Luke 4:18
"The Spirit of the Lord is upon me,
  because he has anointed me
    to bring glad tidings to the poor."
How can you bring good news to those who are sick, lonely, or in need in other ways?

_____

_____

_____

What can you do to show those who are blind to the needs of others how to love as Jesus loves?

_____

_____

_____

Liturgy of the Eucharist

In the Liturgy of the Eucharist, you are united with Jesus and his sacrifice. You receive the Body and Blood of Christ under the appearance of bread and wine. When you share in the Eucharist, God unites you to himself and others. You are one with all who belong to the Church on earth, in heaven, and in purgatory. The Eucharist nourishes you to live out the Word of God you have heard proclaimed. In every liturgy of the Church, God the Father is blessed and adored as the source of all blessings we have received through his Son in order to make us his children through the Holy Spirit.

The Order of Mass

✦ Number the parts of the Mass in the correct order. Then write LW if it is from the Liturgy of the Word or LE if it is from the Liturgy of the Eucharist.

_____ Homily   _____

_____ Eucharistic Prayer   _____

_____ Prayer over the Offerings   _____

_____ Gospel Reading   _____

_____ Second Reading   _____

_____ Presentation and Preparation of the Gifts   _____

_____ Prayer of the Faithful   _____

All That We Have!

If you really care about something at school—such as chorus, drama, or a sports team—you get involved. In the same way, caring members of God's family get involved in causes that promote the love of God and others. As fully initiated Christians we belong to the People of God, which makes it part of our mission to care for people. We are all valuable members of the Body of Christ.

During the Liturgy of the Eucharist, we unite our sacrifices to the sacrifice of Jesus. We offer our struggles, successes, and services to the Father. At Mass we pray for the needs of the Church and the world, and for the coming of the kingdom.

By offering ourselves and praying for the needs of others, we participate in the best way possible. We show how much we trust the power and goodness that comes to us in Holy Communion. Since the moments spent celebrating the Eucharist are so important, it is important to respond with the community, to pray and sing reverently, and to receive Holy Communion.

When Things Go Wrong

As you prepare to become a confirmed Catholic, think about the role you play in the community of faith. You are part of a grace-filled Church that is united around the Eucharist and worships the Father. Because our Church is human it is capable of sin. Sin is something we do or fail to do that is contradictory to God's law. It is an offense against God, and harms our relationships with him. **Mortal sin,** which breaks our relationships with God, must be confessed in the Sacrament of Penance. Mortal sins are sins that we commit when

- we do something that is seriously wrong.

- we know it is seriously wrong, and

- we freely and willingly choose to do it.

A **venial sin** is a less serious offense that weakens our relationships with God. When we are repentant, we can be forgiven by prayer, good actions, and receiving the Eucharist. But it is recommended that you confess venial sins in the Sacrament of Penance.

Just as the goodness of all in the community strengthens the Body of Christ, so does each of our sins hurt and weaken it. Sin brings division and causes us to be at odds with ourselves, others, and God. When we are wounded by sin, Christ heals us through the Sacrament of Penance.

Like a peacemaker who steps in to break up a fight or an argument, Christ came to bring people together, to heal the brokenhearted, and to restore what was lost by sin. Christ challenges us to forgive one another as he forgives us, and he encourages us to seek forgiveness from him and others. The strength to be healers is given to us by Christ through the Holy Spirit.

How We Can Be Healers

◆ Read these stories. Determine who is a healer and who is not.

Bill overheard Steve being corrected by his teacher for trying to steal from another student's desk. When Bill got to the cafeteria, his classmates wanted to know where Steve was. Bill said that Steve was busy and changed the subject. Is Bill a healer? Why or why not?

_____

_____

Beth made fun of Ann in front of her friends by mocking the way she sang at practice. Later, Beth came and apologized. Ann told her coldly, "Sorry isn't enough," and walked away. Is Beth a healer? Why or why not?

_____

Is Ann a healer? Why or why not?

_____

Spirit-Filled People

Carlos Rodriguez was born in Caguas, Puerto Rico in 1918. He suffered a tremendous setback at age six when his father's store and his family's home were destroyed in a fire.

When Carlos was in high school, he began to develop health problems that would last his whole life. He dropped out of college because of his illness, but he never stopped reading and learning.

His great love was to help people understand and love the Mass and the sacraments. Long before the reforms of the Second Vatican Council, Carlos promoted liturgical renewal, which included celebrating the Mass in Spanish so that people could better understand it. Many people began to experience a renewed faith because of Carlos's teaching and the integrity with which he served the Church and others.

He died of cancer in 1963. In 1999 Pope John Paul II declared him blessed for the example of his life and his dedication to the liturgy. Being named blessed is the last stage before being declared a saint.

For seven happy years, Jane de Chantal managed the castle of her husband, Baron Christophe de Rabutin-Chantal. Each day she gathered her family for Mass and supervised the household and her children's education. She fed the poor and showed her children how to love others.

Then Jane's secure home was torn by tragedy. Christophe was killed by another man in a hunting accident. She tried to be positive and forgiving, but it was very hard.

One day she met Bishop Francis de Sales. She celebrated the Sacrament of Penance with him and told him about her life. Francis told her that she must trust God still more and forgive the man who had accidentally killed her husband. Jane's deep faith helped her to forgive the one who had hurt her most. Eventually she became a godparent for the man's child. She felt the peace of Christ that comes from a forgiving heart. Later, along with Francis de Sales, Jane founded the Sisters of the Visitation. The Church declared her a saint for her holiness.

❖ The Sacrament of Penance

Like Jane de Chantal, we may find it difficult to forgive those who have hurt us. But we can find healing if we choose to forgive. Likewise, we will be happier if we ask Jesus to forgive us our own sins. In the Sacrament of Penance, we encounter Jesus and ask him to forgive our sins through the priest. We trust in God's mercy and in the forgiveness of others who belong to the community of faith.

The priest represents Jesus and the forgiving community. From him we receive **absolution,** our sins are forgiven, and the Church grows stronger and closer together. The divisions caused by our selfishness are healed, and the bonds of the community are strengthened. The priest is bound by the seal of confession never to reveal what anyone confesses.

For Confirmation: Celebrating Penance

Plan to celebrate the Sacrament of Penance during your time of preparation for Confirmation. Review the process for celebrating the sacrament in the Things Every Catholic Should Know section at the back of your book.

Act of Contrition

We want to lead lives of compassion and kindness. But sometimes we do something we know is wrong. We feel sad and guilty and want everything to be made right. With this prayer we call on God's mercy and forgiveness.

My God,

I am sorry for my sins with all my heart.

In choosing to do wrong

and failing to do good,

I have sinned against you

whom I should love above all things.

I firmly intend, with your help,

to do penance,

to sin no more,

and to avoid whatever leads me to sin.

Our Savior Jesus Christ

suffered and died for us.

In his name, my God, have mercy.

Amen.

Now spend some time with God. Ask him for the help you need to avoid what leads to sin and for the strength to ask forgiveness when you've done something wrong. Thank him in your own words for the forgiveness he offers.

SUMMARY

Remember

How do the Sacraments of Eucharist and Penance unite the Christian community?
In the Eucharist we celebrate the mystery of Jesus' sacrifice of love and the holy meal that unites us in the Body of Christ. Through the Sacrament of Penance our sins are forgiven, and we are reconciled with God, the community, and ourselves.

What are the two main parts of the Mass?
The Liturgy of the Word and the Liturgy of the Eucharist are the main parts of the Mass. God's Word and Christ's Body and Blood unite and nourish us as people of God.

Why do we offer ourselves in the Eucharist?
We participate fully in the Eucharist when we offer ourselves and pray for the needs of others. We show how much we trust the power and goodness that comes to us. We do this when we respond, pray, sing, and receive Holy Communion.

How does sin weaken the Body of Christ?
Just as the goodness of all in the community strengthens the Church, so does each of our offenses hurt and weaken it. Sin brings division and causes us to be at odds with ourselves, others, and God. Christ heals our sins through the Sacrament of Penance.

Words to Know

absolution

Liturgy of the Eucharist

Liturgy of the Word

mortal sin

Paschal Mystery

venial sin

Respond

Use your journal to enter more deeply into this chapter. Begin with the prayer on page 5 in your journal. Then quietly spend time on journal pages 36–38.

Reach Out

1. Find out when the priests or extraordinary ministers of the Eucharist bring the Eucharist to members of your parish who are ill.

REVIEW

Finding the Hidden Sacrament

Fill in the blank lines. The boxed letters will spell the sacrament that each sentence describes. Write the name of the sacrament on the last blank line.

1. It helps us __ ☐ __ __ love like our favorite clothes.

2. In it we share in the very life of __ __ __ ☐ __.

3. It helps us live lives of __ __ __ ☐ __.

4. In this sacrament Jesus becomes present through the power of the ☐ __ __ __ __ __ __ __ __ __ __.

5. Jesus' Body and Blood take the appearance of __ __ __ ☐ __ and wine.

6. The __ __ __ ☐ __ __ works in the community gathered for this sacrament.

7. It __ __ __ __ ☐ __ __ __ __ us as people of God.

8. The Word of God proclaimed in this sacrament is the ☐ __ __ __ all over the world.

9. When we share in it, God unites us to himself and __ ☐ __ __ __ __.

_____

Checking the Facts

Place a check mark by the true statements.

____ **1.** When we willingly do something seriously wrong, we commit a mortal sin.

____ **2.** Venial sins are just as serious as mortal sins.

____ **3.** Members of Jesus' community are "one body."

____ **4.** The Holy Spirit does not make Jesus present in the world.

____ **5.** The Spirit makes you one with Jesus.

____ **6.** The Liturgy of the Word and the Liturgy of the Eucharist are the two main parts of the Mass.

____ **7.** You pray only for your own needs at Mass.

____ **8.** It is not important to pray, sing, or respond during Mass.

____ **9.** A confirmed Christian is part of a community that is without grace.

____ **10.** Our sins are forgiven when we receive absolution.

Matching Meaningful Terms

For each definition write the letter of the word that matches it best.

a. mortal sin	**d.** Paschal Mystery
b. absolution	**e.** venial sin
c. Liturgy of the Word	**f.** Liturgy of the Eucharist

____ **1.** the mystery of Jesus' life, death, and Resurrection

____ **2.** unites us in one faith to believe in one God

____ **3.** unites us with Jesus and his sacrifice

____ **4.** must be confessed in the Sacrament of Penance

____ **5.** the forgiveness of sins

____ **6.** lesser sins

Confirmed *in* Grace

What can you do now that you couldn't do when you were seven? How are things different for you now? What do you like best about who you are now?

Lord,
send us your
Holy Spirit
to help us
walk in unity
of faith
and grow in
the strength
of his love
to the full
stature of
Christ.

*The Rite of
Confirmation*

Baptized in the Holy Spirit

While Apollos was in Corinth, Paul traveled through the interior of the country and came [down] to Ephesus where he found some disciples. He said to them, "Did you receive the holy Spirit when you became believers?" They answered him, "We have never even heard that there is a holy Spirit." He said, "How were you baptized?" They replied, "With the baptism of John." Paul then said, "John baptized with a baptism of repentance, telling the people to believe in the one who was to come after him, that is, in Jesus." When they heard this, they were baptized in the name of the Lord Jesus. And when Paul laid [his] hands on them, the holy Spirit came upon them, and they spoke in tongues and prophesied.

Acts of the Apostles 19:1–6

ART Link

❖ *Understanding Scripture*

Paul's mission was to preach the Good News of Jesus to the Gentiles. In Acts of the Apostles 19:1–6, he comes upon some Jews who had been followers of John the Baptist and then followers of Jesus. But they had only been baptized by John, as Jesus had been. Their baptism of repentance by John needed to be completed by Baptism into the life, death, and Resurrection of Jesus. With this Baptism they would receive the Holy Spirit. After they were baptized in the name of the Lord Jesus, Paul laid his hands on them and they received the Holy Spirit. This gift was expressed in the wondrous acts they were then capable of performing.

Ephesus was a wealthy city and the fourth largest in the Roman Empire. Paul spent two years preaching the Gospel there, first in synagogues and then in the public lecture hall. The library at Ephesus, pictured here, was on the main street and was very important to the city's life. It was the second largest library in the Roman Empire.

❖ *Scripture and You*

You were probably baptized as an infant and haven't thought much about it since then. Like the believers in this reading, you may have taken your Baptism for granted. But in your preparation for Confirmation, you have been thinking more seriously about what your Baptism means to you. You received the Holy Spirit at your Baptism, and he will be strengthened in you through the Sacrament of Confirmation.

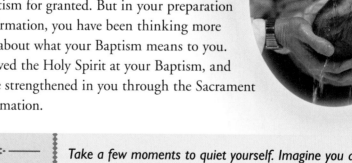

Reflecting *on* **G**od's **W**ord

Take a few moments to quiet yourself. Imagine you are back at the day of your Baptism. Your parents and godparents are there with you as the priest baptizes you. Give thanks to God for your Baptism and the gift of the Holy Spirit you received at that time. Silently speak to God about whatever you would like.

As You Grow

Your life has changed as you've grown older and matured. You've learned things, developed skills, and become more independent. With this growth comes additional privileges and responsibilities. For example, very little was expected of you as a baby. But you were asked to do a great deal more as a six-year-old.

Privileges and Responsibilities

✦ What can you do now that you weren't allowed to do when you were younger?

_____

In what ways do you contribute to your family today that you couldn't in the past?

_____

❖ Spiritual Growth

Just as you grow in strength, size, and intelligence, so are you called to grow in spirit. At Baptism you received the gift of grace, or divine life. As you've grown, you've been called to recognize God's love for you and the great gifts he has given you. Now you are ready to accept the responsibilities and privileges that are yours because of your Baptism. Now you have the opportunity to live out your anointing by the Spirit, and to share more fully in the mission of Jesus.

❖ Confirmation

Confirmation celebrates the gift of the Spirit that you received in Baptism. To be confirmed you must profess your faith, be in the state of grace, and want to receive the sacrament. In Confirmation the Spirit gives you strength to live by God's teachings more fully, to imitate Christ more closely, and to express your faith more courageously. You are bound more closely to the Church in Confirmation so you must be ready to assume the role of disciple and witness to him. The whole community celebrates with you as you commit to Jesus and his Church. The community prays that the Spirit will bless you with the grace you need to grow in Christ. Confirmation is celebrated during the Eucharist to express more clearly the unity of the Sacraments of Initiation.

The bishop is the ordinary minister of Confirmation. He receives the fullness of the sacrament of Holy Orders and shares in the apostolic responsibility and mission of the whole Church.

❖ The Rite of Confirmation

The Rite of Confirmation includes five parts: the presentation of the candidates, homily, renewal of baptismal promises, laying on of hands and anointing with chrism, and general intercessions.

The Mass Begins

Like other liturgical celebrations in which you have participated, the Mass for your Confirmation follows a set pattern. It begins with the opening prayer.

Sending the Spirit

✦ Any of the following can serve as the opening prayer for the Rite of Confirmation. Place a check next to the prayer that best summarizes what your Confirmation means to you.

1. God of power and mercy, send your Holy Spirit to live in our hearts and make us temples of his glory.

2. Lord, fulfill your promise: send the Holy Spirit to make us witnesses before the world to the Good News proclaimed by Jesus Christ our Lord.

3. Lord, send us your Holy Spirit to help us walk in unity of faith and grow in the strength of his love to the full stature of Christ.

4. Lord, fulfill the promise given by your Son and send the Holy Spirit to enlighten our minds and lead us to all truth.

Celebration of the Word

✦ The Holy Spirit brings the Word of God to life for us. In it we find God's will for us. Some suggested readings for Confirmation are listed here. Circle the reading that speaks most to you and write a short summary of it.

First Reading: Isaiah 11:1–4
Isaiah 61:1–3,6,8–9
Ezekiel 36:24–28

Second Reading: Acts of the Apostles 1:3–8
Romans 8:14–17
Ephesians 4:1–6

_____

_____

❖ Presentation of the Candidates

After the readings you are presented to the bishop for Confirmation. You are called by name or as a group. By standing before the bishop, you give witness to your desire to declare yourself a Christian and to live as one. In the Homily the bishop then explains how the Scripture readings reveal a deeper understanding of the mystery of Confirmation.

❖ Renewal of Baptismal Promises

At the end of the Homily, you publicly renew your baptismal promises by standing and affirming your commitment as a follower of Jesus. You are asked if you reject Satan and all his works. You respond, "I do" to this and to basic statements of what we believe.

Strengthen Us

After your profession of faith, the bishop invites everyone to pray with him. He says,

My dear friends:
in Baptism God our Father gave the new birth of eternal life
to his chosen sons and daughters.
Let us pray to our Father
that he will pour out the Holy Spirit
to strengthen his sons and daughters with his gifts
and anoint them to be more like Christ the Son of God.

Promises of the Spirit

✦ Underline the two things in the prayer above that the Spirit does for you in Confirmation.

❖ Come, Holy Spirit

As the bishop extends his hands over you in the Rite of Confirmation, your parents, sponsors, and the entire congregation are united in focusing on one thought: Come, Holy Spirit.

The bishop prays,

All-powerful God, Father of our Lord Jesus Christ,
by water and the Holy Spirit
you freed your sons and daughters from sin
and gave them new life.

Send your Holy Spirit upon them
to be their Helper and Guide.

Give them the spirit of wisdom and understanding,
the spirit of right judgment and courage,
the spirit of knowledge and reverence.

Fill them with the spirit of wonder and awe in your presence.

We ask this through Christ our Lord.

The Spirit's Gifts

✦ Which of the Spirit's gifts listed in the prayer will most help you? In what ways?

_____

_____

_____

_____

Confirmed in the Spirit

In the Rite of Confirmation, you come before the bishop with your sponsor, and your sponsor places his or her hand on your right shoulder. The bishop confirms you by anointing you with chrism.

- You or your sponsor tells the bishop your Confirmation name.
- The bishop traces the Sign of the Cross with chrism on your forehead and says, "[Name], be sealed with the Gift of the Holy Spirit."
- You respond, "Amen."
- Then the bishop extends to you a sign of peace and says, "Peace be with you."
- You respond, "And with your spirit."

With the bishop's anointing you receive an indelible, or permanent, character that signifies the way you are sealed with the gift of the Holy Spirit. The gift helps you become more like Christ and commissions you to live your prophetic mission to be a witness to him in all circumstances and at the very heart of the human community.

❖ The Mass Continues

The Mass continues with intercessions offered for all of our needs. In the liturgy you and the other newly confirmed, who have been united in the gift of the Spirit, are bound together in the worship of the Father through his Son, Jesus Christ. You are joined more closely with one another in praying the Lord's Prayer, in sharing the sign of Christ's peace, and in receiving Holy Communion. When you participate in the Eucharist, you celebrate the life of faith that has been confirmed in you through the action of the Holy Spirit.

❖ The Mass Concludes

The Mass ends with a solemn final blessing, or prayer, over all of the people in the assembly. The bishop extends his hands over all and prays the following prayer or one similar to it.

Bishop: God our Father
made you his children by water
  and the Holy Spirit:
may he bless you
and watch over you with his fatherly love.
Response: Amen.

Bishop: Jesus Christ the Son of God
promised that the Spirit of truth
will be with his Church for ever:
may he bless you and give you courage
in professing the true faith.
Response: Amen.

Bishop: The Holy Spirit
came down upon the disciples
and set their hearts on fire with love:
may he bless you,
keep you one in faith and love
and bring you to the joy of God's kingdom.
Response: Amen.

Bishop: May almighty God bless you,
the Father, and the Son, and the Holy Spirit.
Response: Amen.

✦ Review the prayer of final blessing on page 66. Write what each Person of the Trinity did for us or for the disciples.

_____

_____

_____

Write what each Person of the Trinity will do for us.

_____

_____

_____

❖ *Living Your Commitment*

Having reached the age of reason, when you are anointed, sealed, and blessed in Confirmation, you assume the role of witness to Jesus in the Church and in the world. By cooperating with the Holy Spirit, you will grow in the knowledge and love of Jesus.

A Closing Thought

✦ When you are sealed, you are stamped, or set apart, for God. You belong to God, who will call on you to help achieve his mission.

After you are confirmed, how will people be able to tell from your life that you are a follower of Jesus?

_____

_____

For Confirmation: Novena

Find the Confirmation Novena in the back of the book. Carefully tear it out and fold it. Use it to prepare for your Confirmation.

God's Kind and Generous Love

Leader: As the day of Confirmation approaches, let us listen to God's Word from the Letter to Titus and take some time to pray for one another.

Reader: A Reading from the Letter to Titus.
[A reader from the group reads from Titus 3:4–7.]

All: Thanks be to God.

Leader: Let us pray for all those preparing for Confirmation. May they remain faithful to God, give bold witness to the Gospel, and become heirs in hope of eternal life.

Reader: For all of us, sons and daughters of God, that confirmed by the gift of the Spirit we will give witness to Christ by lives built on faith and love. Let us pray to the Lord.

All: Lord, hear our prayer.

Reader: For our parents and godparents, who lead us in faith, that by word and example they may always encourage us to follow the way of Jesus. Let us pray to the Lord.

All: Lord, hear our prayer.

Reader: For all members of the Church, that God, who gathers us together by the Holy Spirit, may help us grow in unity of faith and love until Jesus, his Son, returns in glory. Let us pray to the Lord.

All: Lord, hear our prayer.

Leader: May the work of the Holy Spirit begun at Pentecost continue to grow in the hearts of all who believe.

All: Amen.

Leader: Let us offer each other a sign of peace.

Summary

Remember

What is the connection between the Sacraments of Baptism and Confirmation?
The Sacrament of Confirmation perfects Baptismal grace, affirms the responsibilities and privileges that you received during Baptism, and celebrates the gift of the Spirit given to you at Baptism.

Why does the Rite of Confirmation take place during a Mass?
When you receive the Eucharist, you participate in and celebrate the faith life that has been confirmed in you through the Holy Spirit. Celebrating Confirmation during the Eucharist expresses the unity of the Sacraments of Initiation.

What are the five parts of the Rite of Confirmation?
The five parts of the Rite of Confirmation are the presentation of the candidates, homily, renewal of baptismal promises, laying on of hands and anointing with chrism, and general intercessions.

What do you express when you stand before the bishop during the presentation of candidates?
When you stand before the bishop, you give witness to your desire to declare yourself ready to be a disciple and witness of Christ and to live according to his example of love for God and others.

What does the bishop do to confirm you?
The bishop anoints you with chrism on the forehead and says: "[Name], be sealed with the Gift of the Holy Spirit."

Respond

Use your journal to enter more deeply into this chapter. Begin with the prayer on page 5 of your journal. Then quietly spend time on journal pages 42–44.

Reach Out

1. Read a biography of a Christian known for his or her faith.

2. Plan a reception with your class to be held immediately after Confirmation. Invite your parents, sponsors, catechists, priests, the bishop, and friends. Prepare thank-you cards, decorations, and refreshments with a Holy Spirit theme.

3. Ask a priest what his anointing at Holy Orders meant to him.

4. Write a paragraph on one of the following topics:
- Confirmation Is a New Beginning
- My Faith Is Important to Me
- My Faith Needs to Grow
- Confirmation Empowers Me

Celebrating Confirmation

Number the steps in the Confirmation Mass in the order they occur.

___ homily

___ readings from Scripture

___ laying on of hands and anointing with chrism

___ general intercessions

___ final blessing

___ renewal of baptismal promises

___ presentation of the candidates

Confirmation Crossing

Use the clues to complete this crossword puzzle about the Rite of Confirmation.

Across

4. The bishop anoints you with this.

6. You become more like Christ when you grow this way.

7. Three of these— Baptism, Confirmation, and the Eucharist— initiate you as a Christian.

8. The Spirit keeps them active in you.

Down

1. This helps celebrate the unity of the Sacraments of Initiation.

2. You declare yourself this.

3. laying on of hands

4. The Spirit helps you become more like him.

5. another word for the permanent character you receive

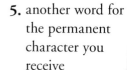

Confirmed *in* Witness

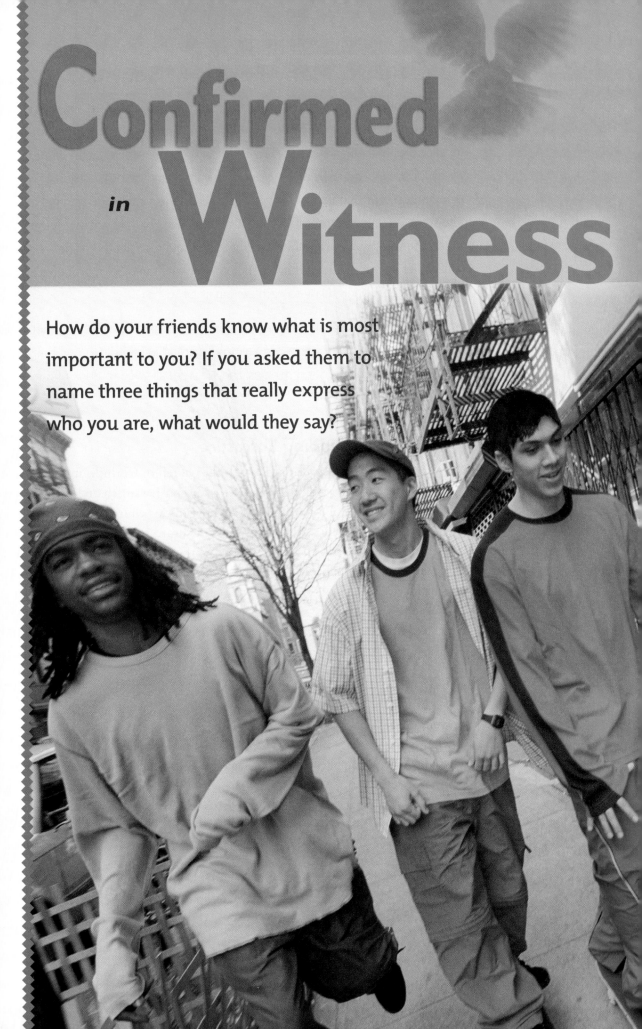

How do your friends know what is most important to you? If you asked them to name three things that really express who you are, what would they say?

One Spirit, Many Forms of Service

There are different kinds of spiritual gifts but the same Spirit; there are different forms of service but the same Lord; there are different workings but the same God who produces all of them in everyone. To each individual the manifestation of the Spirit is given for some benefit. To one is given through the Spirit the expression of wisdom; to another the expression of knowledge according to the same Spirit; to another faith by the same Spirit; to another gifts of healing by the one Spirit; to another mighty deeds; to another prophecy; to another discernment of spirits; to another varieties of tongues; to another interpretation of tongues. But one and the same Spirit produces all of these, distributing them individually to each person as he wishes.

As a body is one though it has many parts, and all the parts of the body, though many, are one body, so also Christ. For in one Spirit we were all baptized into one body, whether Jews or Greeks, slaves or free persons, and we were all given to drink of one Spirit.

1 Corinthians 12:4–13

St. Paul the Apostle, by Nicholas Markell, is an example of a modern icon. An icon is a religious painting of Jesus, Mary, or a saint that attempts to show how the divine life of God can be seen in them. Icons remind us that we are all made in the image of God and called to be changed into his likeness.

❖ Understanding Scripture

The passage you just read deals with the church in Corinth. It was made up of a great variety of people: Romans, Greeks, and Jews; rich and poor; citizens and noncitizens; free and slaves. After Paul began this church in Corinth, he left to begin churches in other cities. When he heard from his friends in Corinth that things were not going well, he wrote them letters such as this one. Paul is reminding everyone that they are very different from one another. But all were baptized into the one Body of Christ. They all have different gifts to share. All of their spiritual gifts were given to them by the Holy Spirit and were meant to build up the community, not to divide it. Whatever their gifts, they are meant to be used for the good of all.

❖ Scripture and You

In your preparation for Confirmation, you have been growing in your understanding of your faith, considering ways you can live as a better follower of Jesus, and thinking about how to use the gifts you have been given. Now is the time to ask yourself, what form of service can I give to others? Don't worry that some people seem to be able to do a lot of things better than you can. Each of us is different, and each of us has been given different gifts to use for the good of all. Think of one of your gifts. How can you best share it with others?

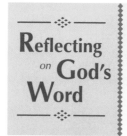

Reflecting *on* **God's Word**

Relax and close your eyes if you like. Reflect on your friends. Think about the different gifts some of them have to offer. Thank God for all this variety. Ask him to help you to use your gifts to the best of your ability.

Ready to Witness

After your Confirmation you may not be exceptionally wiser. You probably won't be speaking in tongues or healing people. You will probably feel about the same as you did before Confirmation. Your growth in the Spirit will be a day-by-day journey. But the same Holy Spirit who came to the early Christians on Pentecost has also strengthened you for your mission.

The time after your Confirmation is especially important. You can fulfill your prophetic mission to be a witness to Christ in all circumstances and at the very heart of the human community. You can participate in the Eucharist, pray, perform works of mercy, and live a courageous Christian life. During this time the community of faith will continue to support you and encourage you to share your gifts and talents in loving service for Christ.

❖ A Plan for Spiritual Growth

To be disciples of Christ and to grow spiritually, we are called to exhibit these same qualities. Here are some suggestions for continuing your spiritual growth. Think about how you will apply them to your life, and make a firm commitment to do so.

Eucharist *Participating in the Eucharist is the most important part of your week.*

- Prepare to offer your problems, struggles, and successes with Christ and to receive him in the Eucharist.
- Pray at the Eucharistic liturgy for a greater love for Christ and others.
- After Mass write in your journal thoughts from the readings or the Homily.

Prayer *Your relationship with God is nurtured through communication.*

- Read about God's love for you in the Scriptures.
- Take time during your day to talk to God.
- Write your reflections in your journal.
- Pray the Rosary.

Works of Charity *Jesus showed us what a life of loving service means.*

- Practice the works of mercy.
- Show concern for those who are poor and in need.
- Be of service at home, in school, and in your parish.

Community *You share a common vision and love for Christ and other members of his body, the Church.*

- Recognize when you need to be reconciled with anyone.
- Take advantage of opportunities to celebrate the Sacrament of Penance.
- Share your faith and grow in it by participating in the parish youth group, Bible Study, or any other parish activity.

Fruits of the Spirit

Healthy trees flourish and bear fruit: apples, oranges, peaches. When you live united to Christ and follow the guidance of the Holy Spirit, your life bears the fruit of good works. You will be aware of God dwelling in you by the joy you experience in doing good. People will recognize God's presence in you by seeing your good works, your love for others, and your service to them.

Saint Paul wrote to the Galatians: "The fruit of the Spirit is love, joy, peace, patience, kindness, generosity, faithfulness, gentleness, self-control" (Galatians 5:22–23). To this list Church Tradition has added goodness, modesty, and chastity. These are the 12 **Fruits of the Holy Spirit.** They are the results of the Spirit's presence and gifts in a believing person. They are also the result of cooperating with God's grace.

Read the following descriptions of the Fruits of the Holy Spirit and the stories that follow. Find evidence of the Fruits of the Holy Spirit in these stories. Think about how people might find evidence of some of them in your life.

❖ Love

Love, or charity, is shown in selfless service to others by your words and actions. Love is a sign that you love God and that you love others as Jesus loves you.

❖ Faithfulness

Keep your promises. You are faithful when you show loyalty to God and to those to whom you have committed yourself. Faithful people are dependable, trustworthy, and obedient.

A Man Who Loved God and Others If you went into the Berard family's hairdressing shop in Manhattan in the early 1800s, you received much more than a shave and a haircut. Pierre Toussaint, an enslaved man who was Catholic, worked for the family and was skilled at his trade. Day after day he listened to people's heartaches and family stories as he cut their hair. Time after time he would speak to his customers in simple language about Jesus, Mary, and the importance of loving others. Pierre was never too tired after work to care for the poor. He used much of the money he made to buy the freedom of other enslaved people rather than spending it to buy his own freedom. Pierre was an ordinary person who showed other ordinary people how to be holy. He was faithful to his baptismal promises. Pierre was a Catholic not only on Sunday, but on every day of the week.

What Can You Contribute?

✦ Practice: Make a list of acts of charity that a young person can perform.

_____ _____

_____ _____

_____ _____

_____

❖ Joy

Joy is deep and constant gladness in the Lord that circumstances cannot destroy. It comes from a good relationship with God and others—a relationship of genuine love.

❖ Modesty

Modesty is moderation in all your actions, especially your conversation and external behavior. Modesty is a sign that you give credit to God for your talents and successes.

A Nurse from God An old woman climbed the last step of the staircase and leaned against the wall, gasping for breath. She knocked on the door, which was opened by a refined, red-haired woman in a gray dress. "Excuse me, ma'am. They said you were a nurse and could help me," said the old lady. "If you can't, they'll send me to die on Blackwell Island."

The old woman said she would pay her when she was able. "Nonsense," said the red-haired woman, whose name was Rose. "If you had the money you could go to the hospital. I help those who can't pay." Rose gently unwrapped the bandage to reveal a cancerous wound on the woman's face. Rose's hand worked quickly to clean the sore.

The old woman commented that Rose was very kind and that she must come from a nice family. "I do come from a nice family," Rose replied, "God's family. You're part of that family too. And in God's family we help one another."

Rose Hawthorne did help the poorest and most unloved of God's family. In the early 1900s she began caring for neglected people in New York who were forced to die on Blackwell Island. Eventually she founded an order of Dominican sisters who cared for incurable cancer patients.

Bringing Goodness to the World

✦ Think of a person you don't know very well. How can you show love for this person this week?

_____

_____

Read 2 Corinthians 9:7. What kind of attitude does Jesus expect from his followers?

_____

❖ Kindness

Kindness is shown by generous acts of service. Kind people are compassionate and considerate. They try to see the best in others.

❖ Goodness

This Fruit of the Holy Spirit flows from God's great love. It is a sign that you love all people without exception and do good to them.

❖ Peace

Jesus said to his disciples on Easter morning, "Peace I give you." A disciple faithful to God's will is serene, not overly anxious or upset. Peace comes from knowing that all will work out well because God is with us.

❖ Patience

We are confronted with difficulties on a daily basis. Patience is love that is willing to endure life's suffering, difficulties, and routine. It means not giving up in difficult situations.

A Mother's Patience "Angelo!" Mama Roncalli wiped her hands on her apron and raised her eyes to heaven. "Dear Lord, what will I do with this boy?"

Angelo looked down at his homework. "I guess I'm not interested in school right now," he said. He glanced enviously out the window to where his brothers and sisters were playing.

But his mother was not persuaded. "You will finish this paper," she insisted. "Then you can go outside." Reluctantly Angelo accepted this disappointment and went to work on the paper.

Decades later Angelo, as Pope John XXIII, would have made his mother very proud. He was well-educated and understood God's people. He called the Second Vatican Council to renew the Church and help it address the concerns of the 20th century. Many of his advisors protested the idea of Church renewal. They were not convinced that renewal was needed. Pope John XXIII accepted their opposition with patience, but he did not give up. He knew that God would guide the Council. Even when Pope John XXIII faced an unfinished Council before he died, he could smile peacefully and say calmly, "God will take care." He was beatified in the year 2000.

A Need for Peace

✦ World peace, family peace, personal peace—which do you see as the greatest need right now? Write one petition expressing your belief.

_____

_____

_____

Imagine you are writing a book for young people your age to help them grow spiritually. It is called *How to Be Patient.* Suggest four ways to practice patience as a Christian youth.

_____

_____

_____

❖ Self-control

You can discipline your physical and emotional desires by being modest and respectful of others. With self-control you can be in charge of your emotions and desires instead of the other way around.

❖ Chastity

Chastity is the integration of your physical sexuality with your spiritual nature. All people, married and single, are called to practice chastity.

A Chaste Couple "There was nothing really extraordinary about our family," Tarcisio Beltrame remembered. "It was really very ordinary, with its own weaknesses." He was speaking on the occasion of the beatification of his parents, Luigi and Maria Beltrame Quattrocchi, on October 21, 2001.

Luigi and Maria married in 1905. They raised four children and also found time to lead active lives of Christian service. At the Mass declaring them blessed, Pope John Paul II said, "They lived an ordinary life in an extraordinary way. The richness of faith and married love shown by Luigi and Maria is a living demonstration of what the Second Vatican Council said about all the faithful being called to holiness."

Through their love for each other, Luigi and Maria gave to others. Together they were a family that was open to prayer, solidarity with the poor, and friendship. The pope decided that they should share the same feast day. He chose November 25, their wedding anniversary.

Living a Chaste Life

✦ How can Scripture, prayer, the sacraments, or the examples of other Christians help you to practice self-control or chastity?

_____

_____

❖ Generosity

Generosity is a willingness to give even at a cost to yourself. It expresses concern for meeting the needs of others even if it means sacrificing something of your own.

❖ Gentleness

Strength tempered by love leads you to be gentle, peaceful, and gracious. A gentle person has the power to forgive instead of getting angry.

Being Generous

✦ What is a way that a young person can show generosity?

_____

_____

For the Least of my People

In the parable of the Last Judgment in Matthew's Gospel, Jesus tells us that everything we do for those in need, we also do for him. Reflect on these phrases from Matthew 25:31–46. How can you best serve those in need as Jesus asks you?

"Come, you who are blessed by my Father. Inherit the kingdom prepared for you from the foundation of the world."

Jesus has planned good things for you. What can you do to be called blessed by Jesus' Father?

How can you meet the needs of those around you?

"For I was hungry and you gave me food, I was thirsty and you gave me drink, a stranger and you welcomed me, naked and you clothed me, ill and you cared for me, in prison and you visited me."

In what ways have you begun to do this? How can you continue to care for those in need?

"And the king will say to them in reply, 'Amen, I say to you, whatever you did for one of these least brothers of mine, you did for me.'"

Spend a few moments asking Jesus to help you serve him in all who are in need. Tell him you are ready to live out your responsibilities as a confirmed Catholic.

SUMMARY

Remember

How can you nurture your relationship with God?

Your relationship with God can grow through communication—talking and listening to him in prayer. Reading the Bible and recording your thoughts in your journal will help improve your prayer life.

How can you recognize the Fruits of the Holy Spirit?

You can recognize the Fruits of the Holy Spirit in yourself by the happiness you experience in doing good. Others become aware of the Spirit's presence in you by witnessing your good works.

How do we make the most of the Fruits of the Spirit in our lives?

The Fruits of the Spirit are the result of the Spirit's presence and gifts in a person who believes. They are the result of cooperating with God's grace.

Words to Know

Fruits of the Holy Spirit

Respond

Use your journal to enter more deeply into this chapter. Begin with the prayer on page 5 of your journal. Then quietly spend time on journal pages 48–50.

Reach Out

1. Look up other signs of the Spirit found in 1 Timothy 4:12; 6:11; 2 Timothy 2:22–24; 1 Peter 3:8; and Ephesians 5:8–9. Write how some of these are evident in your parish community. Offer to allow some of your thoughts to be printed in the parish bulletin.

2. Develop a personal plan for spiritual growth based on the content of page 73. Show it to your sponsor, your parents, your pastor, or another adult Christian. Follow their suggestions for ways to develop your spiritual life.

3. As a fully initiated Catholic, you will be thinking about your mission, or vocation, in life. Interview a single person, a married couple (perhaps your parents), and a priest or sister about how they have experienced their call.

REVIEW

Searching for Fruit

Circle the hidden Fruits of the Holy Spirit.

goodness   love   joy

modesty   gentleness   self-control

kindness   peace   chastity

faithfulness   generosity   patience

```
L X K C O N G C R Y S X A C B
E O D I J J H K T F S D K H E
T F R I N Y C I O P E M E A I
G P S T P D S B A I N C S S B
P O Q N N O N T U W E R Y T F
P M Q E R O I E V P L E E I Y
Q F L E Z E C I S B T C Q T R
M U N B N C Y F E S N A I Y Z
E E Q C X I X T L H E E T T H
G O E U G X K N S E G P P Y O
Y G O O D N E S S E S U O H G
O X L S X C K O N C D J Y H L
E V O L A H C E O H E O A A Z
S S E N L U F H T I A F M Y K
G M B P K F R K B B U H A P I
```

Describing a Christian

Pretend you are a reporter. Briefly summarize a day in the life of a Christian your age. The person can be real or fictional.

_____

_____

_____

_____

Make it True

Write *T* for *True* or *F* for *False*. Then fix the false statements to make them true.

1. _____ Jesus' example of how to live included practicing acts of mercy and caring for the poor.

_____

2. _____ Your relationship with God is nurtured through communication.

_____

3. _____ Paul's letter to the Galatians names all of the fruits recognized by the Church today.

_____

4. _____ Faithfulness is the sign that you love God and that you love others as Jesus did.

_____

5. _____ Modesty is moderation in all your actions.

_____

6. _____ Kindness is shown by serving others with generosity.

_____

7. _____ Modesty shows that you love all people without exception and do good to them.

_____

8. _____ Peace comes from not knowing that things will work out.

_____

9. _____ Patience is love that is willing to endure suffering.

_____

10. _____ You can't discipline your physical desire by being modest and respectful to others.

_____

Things Every Catholic Should Know

Living Our Faith

❖ The Ten Commandments

As believers in Jesus Christ, we are called to a new life and are asked to make moral choices that keep us united with God. With the help and grace of the Holy Spirit, we can choose ways to act to remain friends with God, to help other people, and to fulfill our prophetic mission to be witnesses to Christ in all circumstances and at the very heart of the human community.

The Ten Commandments are a special expression of natural law made known to us by God's revelation and by human reason. They guide us in making choices that allow us to live as God wants us to live. The first three commandments tell us how to love God; the rest show us how to love our neighbor.

1. I am the Lord your God: you shall not have strange gods before me.
2. You shall not take the name of the Lord your God in vain.
3. Remember to keep holy the Lord's Day.
4. Honor your father and your mother.
5. You shall not kill.
6. You shall not commit adultery.
7. You shall not steal.
8. You shall not bear false witness against your neighbor.
9. You shall not covet your neighbor's wife.
10. You shall not covet your neighbor's goods.

❖ The Great Commandment

The Ten Commandments are fulfilled in Jesus' Great Commandment: "You shall love God with all your heart, with all your soul, with all your mind, and with all your strength. . . . You shall love your neighbor as yourself."

adapted from Mark 12:30–31

❖ The New Commandment

Before his death on the cross, Jesus gave his disciples a new commandment: "Love one another. As I have loved you, so you also should love one another."

John 13:34

❖ The Beatitudes

The Beatitudes are the teachings of Jesus in the Sermon on the Mount (Matthew 5:3–10).

Jesus teaches us that if we live according to the Beatitudes, we will live a happy Christian life. The Beatitudes fulfill God's promises made to Abraham and his descendants and describe the rewards that will be ours as loyal followers of Christ.

Blessed are the poor in spirit, for theirs is the kingdom of heaven.

Blessed are they who mourn, for they will be comforted.

Blessed are the meek, for they will inherit the land.

Blessed are they who hunger and thirst for righteousness, for they will be satisfied.

Blessed are the merciful, for they will be shown mercy.

Blessed are the clean of heart, for they will see God.

Blessed are the peacemakers, for they will be called children of God.

Blessed are those who are persecuted for the sake of righteousness, for theirs is the kingdom of heaven.

❖ Works of Mercy

The corporal and spiritual works of mercy are actions that extend God's compassion and mercy to those in need.

Corporal Works of Mercy

The corporal works of mercy are kind acts by which we help our neighbors with their material and physical needs. They include

feed the hungry   shelter the homeless
clothe the naked   visit the sick and
bury the dead   imprisoned
give alms to the poor

Spiritual Works of Mercy

The spiritual works of mercy are acts of compassion that aim at people's emotional and spiritual needs. They include

instruct   advise
console   comfort
forgive   bear wrongs patiently

❖ Precepts of the Church

The Precepts of the Church describe the minimum effort we must make in prayer and in living a moral life. All Catholics are called to move beyond the minimum by growing in love of God and love of neighbor. The Precepts are as follows:

1. attendance at Mass on Sundays and Holy Days of Obligation

2. confession of sins at least once a year

3. reception of Holy Communion at least once a year during the Easter season

4. observance of the days of fast and abstinence

5. providing for the needs of the Church

❖ Days of Fast (for Adults)

Ash Wednesday   Good Friday

❖ Days of Abstinence
(for all those over 14)

Ash Wednesday   All Fridays in Lent

❖ Holy Days of Obligation

Holy Days of Obligation are the days other than Sundays on which we celebrate the great things God has done for us through Jesus and the saints. On Holy Days of Obligation, Catholics are obliged to attend Mass. Six Holy Days of Obligation are celebrated in the United States.

Mary, Mother of God—January 1

Ascension—Forty days after Easter
(for those dioceses that do not celebrate the Ascension on the seventh Sunday of Easter)

Assumption of the
Blessed Virgin Mary—August 15

All Saints—November 1

Immaculate Conception—December 8

Nativity of Our
Lord Jesus Christ—December 25

❖ Virtues

Virtues are gifts from God that lead us to live in a close relationship with him. Virtues are like good habits. They need to be used; they can be lost if they are neglected. The three most important virtues are called theological virtues because they come from God and lead to God. The cardinal virtues are human virtues, acquired by education and good actions. They are named for the Latin word for "hinge" (cardo), meaning "that on which other things depend."

Theological Virtues

faith   hope
charity

Cardinal Virtues

prudence   justice

fortitude   temperance

❖ Gifts of the Holy Spirit

The Holy Spirit makes it possible for us to do what God the Father asks of us by giving us many gifts. They include the following:

wisdom   right judgment

knowledge   understanding

courage   wonder and awe

reverence

❖ Fruits of the Holy Spirit

The Fruits of the Holy Spirit are examples of the way we find ourselves acting because God is alive in us. They include the following:

love	joy	peace
kindness	generosity	goodness
gentleness	self-control	modesty
faithfulness	chastity	patience

❖ Making Good Choices

Our conscience is the inner voice that helps us know the law God has placed in our hearts. Our conscience helps us judge the moral qualities of our own actions. It guides us to do good and avoid evil.

The Holy Spirit can help us form a good conscience. We form our conscience by studying the teachings of the Church and following the guidance of our parents and pastoral leaders.

God has given every human being freedom of choice. This does not mean that we have the right to do whatever we please. We can live in true freedom if we cooperate with the Holy Spirit, who gives us the virtue of prudence. This virtue helps us recognize what is good in every situation and make correct choices. The Holy Spirit gives us the gifts of wisdom and understanding to help us make the right choices in life in relationship to God and others. The gift of counsel helps us reflect on making correct choices in life.

❖ An Examination of Conscience

An examination of conscience is the act of prayerfully looking into our hearts to ask how we have hurt our relationships with God and other people through our thoughts, words, and actions. We reflect on the Ten Commandments and the teachings of the Church. The questions below will help us in our examination of conscience.

My Relationship with God

What steps am I taking to help myself grow closer to God and others? Do I turn to God often during the day, especially when I am tempted?

Do I participate at Mass with attention and devotion on Sundays and Holy Days? Do I pray often and read the Bible?

Do I use God's name or the name of Jesus, Mary, and the saints with love and reverence?

My Relationship with Family, Friends, and Neighbors

Have I set a bad example through my words or actions? Do I treat others fairly? Do I spread stories that hurt other people?

Am I loving of those in my family? Am I respectful to my neighbors, friends, and those in authority?

Do I show respect for my body and for the bodies of others? Do I keep away from forms of entertainment that do not respect God's gift of sexuality?

Have I taken or damaged anything that did not belong to me? Have I cheated, copied homework, or lied?

Do I quarrel with others just so I can get my own way? Do I insult others to try to make them think they are less than I am? Do I hold grudges and try to hurt people who I think have hurt me?

❖ How to Make a Good Confession

An examination of conscience is an important part of preparing for the Sacrament of Penance. The Sacrament of Penance includes the following steps:

1. The priest greets us and we pray the Sign of the Cross. He may read God's Word with us.

2. We confess our sins. The priest may help and counsel us.

3. The priest gives us a penance to perform. Penance is prayers to be prayed, an act of kindness, or both.

4. The priest asks us to express our sorrow, usually by reciting the Act of Contrition.

5. We receive absolution. The priest says, "I absolve you from your sins in the name of the Father, and of the Son, and of the Holy Spirit." We respond, "Amen."

6. The priest dismisses us by saying, "Go in peace." We go forth to perform the act of penance he has given us.

❖ Showing Our Love for the World

In the story of the Good Samaritan *(Luke 10:29–37)*, Jesus makes clear our responsibility to care for those in need. The Catholic Church teaches this responsibility in the following themes of Catholic Social Teaching.

Life and Dignity of the Human Person

All human life is sacred, and all people must be respected and valued over material goods. We are called to ask whether our actions as a society respect or threaten the life and dignity of the human person.

Call to Family, Community, and Participation

Participation in family and community is central to our faith and a healthy society. Families must be supported so that people can participate in society, build a community spirit, and promote the well-being of all, especially the poor and vulnerable.

Rights and Responsibilities

Every person has a right to life as well as a right to those things required for human decency. As Catholics, we have a responsibility to protect these basic human rights in order to achieve a healthy society.

Option for the Poor and Vulnerable

In our world many people are very rich while at the same time many are extremely poor. As Catholics we are called to pay special attention to the needs of the poor by defending and promoting their dignity and meeting their immediate material needs.

The Dignity of Work and the Rights of Workers

The Catholic Church teaches that the basic rights of workers must be respected: the right to productive work, fair wages, and private property; and the right to organize, join unions, and pursue economic opportunity. Catholics believe that the economy is meant to serve people and that work is not merely a way to make a living, but an important way in which we participate in God's creation.

Solidarity

Because God is our Father, we are all brothers and sisters with the responsibility to care for one another. Solidarity is the attitude that leads Christians to share spiritual and material goods. Solidarity unites rich and poor, weak and strong, and helps create a society that recognizes that we all depend upon one another.

Care for God's Creation

God is the creator of all people and all things, and he wants us to enjoy his creation. The responsibility to care for all God has made is a requirement of our faith.

Celebrating Our Faith

❖ Celebrating the Lord's Day

Sunday is the day on which we celebrate the Resurrection of Jesus. Sunday is the Lord's Day. We gather for Mass, rest from work, and perform works of mercy. People from all over the world gather at God's Eucharistic table as brothers and sisters on the Lord's Day.

The Order of Mass

The Mass is the high point of the Christian life, and it always follows a set order.

Introductory Rites

We prepare to celebrate the Eucharist.

Entrance Chant

We gather as a community praising God in song.

Greeting

We pray the Sign of the Cross, recognizing the presence of Christ in the community.

Penitential Act

We remember our sins and ask God for mercy.

Gloria

We praise God in song.

Collect Prayer

The priest gathers all of our prayers into one.

Liturgy of the Word

We hear the story of God's plan for salvation.

First Reading

We listen to God's Word, usually from the Old Testament.

Responsorial Psalm

We respond to God's Word in song.

Second Reading

We listen to God's Word from the New Testament.

Gospel Acclamation

We sing "Alleluia!" to praise God for the Good News. During Lent we sing a different acclamation.

Gospel Reading

We stand to acclaim Christ present in the Gospel.

Homily

The priest or deacon explains God's Word.

Profession of Faith

We proclaim our faith through the Creed.

Prayer of the Faithful

We pray for our needs and the needs of others.

Liturgy of the Eucharist

We celebrate the meal that Jesus instituted at the Last Supper and remember the sacrifice he made for us.

Presentation and Preparation of the Gifts

We bring gifts of bread and wine to the altar.

Prayer over the Offerings

The priest prays that God will accept our sacrifice.

Eucharistic Prayer

This prayer of thanksgiving is the center and high point of the entire celebration.

Preface—We give thanks and praise to God.

Preface Acclamation (or Holy, Holy, Holy)— We sing an acclamation of praise.

Institution Narrative—The bread and wine become the Body and Blood of Jesus Christ.

The Mystery of Faith—We proclaim Jesus' Death and Resurrection.

Communion Rite

We prepare to receive the Body and Blood of Jesus Christ.

The Lord's Prayer

We pray the Our Father.

Sign of Peace

We offer one another Christ's peace.

Lamb of God

We pray for forgiveness, mercy, and peace.

Communion

We receive the Body and Blood of Jesus Christ.

Prayer after Communion

We pray that the Eucharist will strengthen us to live as Jesus Christ did.

Concluding Rites

At the conclusion of Mass we are blessed and sent forth.

Final Blessing

We receive God's blessing.

Dismissal

We go in peace to glorify the Lord in our lives.

❖ The Seven Sacraments

Jesus touches our lives through the sacraments. In the sacraments physical objects—water, bread and wine, oil, and others—are the signs of Jesus' presence.

Sacraments of Initiation

These sacraments lay the foundation of every Christian life.

Baptism

In Baptism we are born into new life in Christ. Baptism takes away original sin and makes us members of the Church. Its sign is the pouring of water.

Confirmation

Confirmation seals our life of faith in Jesus. Its signs are the laying on of hands on a person's head, most often by a bishop, and the anointing with oil. Like Baptism, it is received only once.

Eucharist

The Eucharist nourishes our life of faith. We receive the Body and Blood of Christ under the appearance of bread and wine.

Sacraments of Healing

These sacraments celebrate the healing power of Jesus.

Penance

Through Penance we receive God's forgiveness. Forgiveness requires being sorry for our sins. In Penance we receive Jesus' healing grace through absolution by the priest. The signs of this sacrament are our confession of sins, our repentance and satisfaction, and the words of absolution.

Anointing of the Sick

This sacrament unites a sick person's sufferings with those of Jesus. Oil, a symbol of strength, is the sign of this sacrament. A person is anointed with oil and receives the laying on of hands from a priest.

Sacraments at the Service of Communion

These sacraments help members serve the community.

Matrimony

In Matrimony, a baptized man and woman are united with each other as a sign of the unity between Jesus and his Church. Matrimony requires the consent of the couple, as expressed in the marriage promises. The couple are the sign of this sacrament.

Holy Orders

In Holy Orders, men are ordained priests to be leaders of the community or deacons to be reminders of our baptismal call to serve others. The signs of this sacrament are the laying on of hands and the prayer asking God for the outpouring of the Holy Spirit by the bishop.

Devotions of Our Faith

❖ *Stations of the Cross*

The 14 Stations of the Cross represent events from Jesus' passion and death. At each station, we use our senses and imaginations to prayerfully reflect upon the mystery of Jesus' suffering, death, and Resurrection.

1. Jesus Is Condemned to Death.
   Pontius Pilate condemns Jesus to death.

2. Jesus Takes Up His Cross.
   Jesus willingly accepts and patiently bears his cross.

3. Jesus Falls the First Time.
   Weakened by torments and by loss of blood, Jesus falls beneath his cross.

4. Jesus Meets His Sorrowful Mother.
   Jesus meets his mother, Mary, who is filled with grief.

5. Simon of Cyrene Helps Jesus Carry the Cross.
   Soldiers force Simon of Cyrene to carry the cross.

6. Veronica Wipes the Face of Jesus.
   Veronica steps through the crowd to wipe the face of Jesus.

7. Jesus Falls a Second Time.
   Jesus falls beneath the weight of the cross a second time.

8. Jesus Meets the Women of Jerusalem.
   Jesus tells the women not to weep for him but for themselves and for their children.

9. Jesus Falls the Third Time.
   Weakened almost to the point of death, Jesus falls a third time.

10. Jesus is Stripped of His Garments.
    The soldiers strip Jesus of his garments, treating him as a common criminal.

11. Jesus Is Nailed to the Cross.
    Jesus' hands and feet are nailed to the cross.

12. Jesus Dies on the Cross.
    After suffering greatly on the cross, Jesus bows his head and dies.

13. Jesus Is Taken Down from the Cross.
    The lifeless body of Jesus is tenderly placed in the arms of Mary, his mother.

14. Jesus Is Laid in the Tomb.
    Jesus' disciples place his body in the tomb.

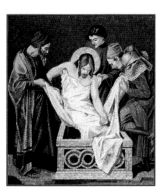

The closing prayer—sometimes included as a 15th station—reflects on the Resurrection of Jesus.

❖ Rosary

The Rosary helps us pray to Jesus through Mary. When we pray the Rosary, we think about the special events, or mysteries, in the lives of Jesus and Mary.

The Rosary is made up of a string of beads and a crucifix. We hold the crucifix in our hand as we pray the Sign of the Cross. Then we pray the Apostles' Creed.

Between the crucifix and the medal of Mary, there is a single bead, followed by a set of three beads and another single bead. We pray the Lord's Prayer as we hold the first single bead, and a Hail Mary at each bead in the set of three that follows. Then we pray the Glory Be to the Father. On the next single bead we think about the first mystery and pray the Lord's Prayer.

There are five sets of ten beads; each set is called a decade. We pray a Hail Mary on each bead of a decade as we reflect on a particular mystery in the lives of Jesus and Mary. The Glory Be to the Father is prayed at the end of each set. Between sets is a single bead on which we think about one of the mysteries and pray the Lord's Prayer. We end by holding the crucifix in our hands as we pray the Sign of the Cross.

Praying the Rosary

1. Pray the Sign of the Cross and the Apostles' Creed.

2. Pray the Lord's Prayer.

3. Pray three Hail Marys and one Glory Be to the Father.

4. Think about the first mystery. Pray the Lord's Prayer.

5. Pray ten Hail Marys and one Glory Be to the Father.

6. Think about the second mystery. Pray the Lord's Prayer.

7. Pray ten Hail Marys and one Glory Be to the Father.

8. Think about the third mystery. Pray the Lord's Prayer.

9. Pray ten Hail Marys and one Glory Be to the Father.

10. Think about the fourth mystery. Pray the Lord's Prayer.

11. Pray ten Hail Marys and one Glory Be to the Father.

12. Think about the fifth mystery. Pray the Lord's Prayer.

13. Pray ten Hail Marys and one Glory Be to the Father.

14. Pray the Sign of the Cross.

The Mysteries of the Rosary

The Church has used three sets of mysteries for many years. In 2002, Pope John Paul II proposed a fourth set of mysteries, the Mysteries of Light or Luminous Mysteries. According to his suggestion, the mysteries might be prayed on the following days: the Joyful Mysteries on Monday and Saturday, the Sorrowful Mysteries on Tuesday and Friday, the Glorious Mysteries on Wednesday and Sunday, and the Luminous Mysteries on Thursday.

The Joyful Mysteries

1. The Annunciation
   Mary learns that she has been chosen to be the mother of Jesus.

2. The Visitation
   Mary visits Elizabeth, who tells her that she will always be remembered.

3. The Nativity
   Jesus is born in a stable in Bethlehem.

4. The Presentation
   Mary and Joseph bring the infant Jesus to the Temple to present him to God.

5. The Finding of Jesus in the Temple
   Jesus is found in the Temple discussing his faith with the teachers.

The Luminous Mysteries

1. The Baptism of Jesus in the River Jordan
   God the Father proclaims that Jesus is his beloved Son.

2. The Wedding Feast at Cana
   At Mary's request, Jesus performs his first miracle.

3. The Proclamation of the Kingdom of God
   Jesus calls all to conversion and service to the Kingdom.

4. The Transfiguration of Jesus
   Jesus is revealed in glory to Peter, James, and John.

5. The Institution of the Eucharist
   Jesus offers his Body and Blood at the Last Supper.

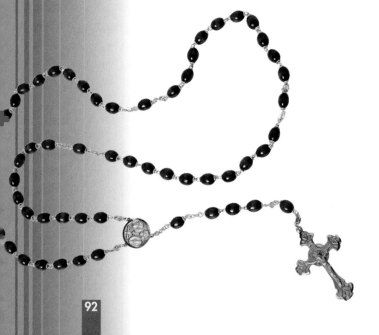

The Sorrowful Mysteries

1. The Agony in the Garden
Jesus prays in the Garden of
Gethsemane on the night before he dies.

2. The Scourging at the Pillar
Jesus is lashed with whips.

3. The Crowning with Thorns
Jesus is mocked and crowned with
thorns.

4. The Carrying of the Cross
Jesus carries the cross that will be used
to crucify him.

5. The Crucifixion
Jesus is nailed to the cross and dies.

The Glorious Mysteries

1. The Resurrection
God the Father raises Jesus from the
dead.

2. The Ascension
Jesus returns to his Father in heaven.

3. The Coming of the Holy Spirit
The Holy Spirit comes to bring new
life to the disciples.

4. The Assumption of Mary
At the end of her life on earth, Mary
is taken body and soul into heaven.

5. The Coronation of Mary
Mary is crowned as Queen of Heaven
and Earth.

Glossary

absolution the forgiveness we receive from God through the priest in the Sacrament of Penance

advocate one who makes an appeal on behalf of another. The word for advocate that John's Gospel uses can also be translated as one who exhorts, who comforts, who helps. It is not as much a name for the Holy Spirit as it is a way of describing how the Spirit continues the work of Jesus after his death and return to the Father.

apostolic one of the four Marks of the Church. The Church is apostolic because it continues to hand on the teaching of the apostles through their successors, the bishops, in union with the successor of Saint Peter, the pope.

Assumption Mary's being taken, body and soul, into heaven. Mary had a special relationship with her Son, Jesus, from the very beginning, when she conceived him. Because of this relationship, she enjoys a special participation in Jesus' Resurrection and has been taken into heaven where she now lives with him. We celebrate this event in the Feast of the Assumption on August 15.

Beatitudes the teachings of Jesus in the Sermon on the Mount in Matthew's Gospel. The Beatitudes are eight ways to live the Christian life. They are the fulfillment of the commandments given to Moses. These teachings present the way to true happiness.

cardinal virtues four virtues or habits that we develop to govern our actions, order our feelings, and guide our conduct according to reason and faith. They are prudence, justice, fortitude, and temperance. They are called cardinal from the Latin word for hinge. It is on them that all the other human virtues depend.

catholic one of the four Marks of the Church. The Church is catholic because Jesus is fully present in it, because it proclaims the fullness of faith, and because Jesus has given the Church to the whole world. The Church is universal.

charity a virtue given to us by God that helps us love him above all things and our neighbor as ourselves

chrism a perfumed oil, consecrated by a bishop, that is used in the Sacraments of Baptism, Confirmation, and Holy Orders. Anointing with chrism signifies the call of the baptized to the threefold ministry of priest, prophet, and king.

Christ a title that means "anointed one." It is from a Greek word that means the same thing as the Hebrew word *Messiah*, or "anointed." It is the name given to Jesus as priest, prophet, and king.

Church the people of God throughout the whole world, or diocese (the local Church), or the assembly of those called together to worship God. The Church is one, holy, catholic, and apostolic.

conscience the inner voice that helps each of us to judge the morality of our own actions. It guides us to follow God's law by doing good and avoiding evil.

corporal works of mercy kind acts by which we help our neighbors with their everyday, material needs. Corporal works of mercy include feeding the hungry, finding a home for the homeless, clothing the naked, visiting the sick and those in prison, giving alms to the poor, and burying the dead.

courage one of the seven Gifts of the Holy Spirit. Courage enables us to stand up for our beliefs and to live as followers of Jesus. With this gift we have the inner strength to do what is right in the face of difficulties and to be faithful in our ordinary duties as Christians.

creation God's act of making everything that exists outside himself. Creation is everything that exists. God said that all of creation is good.

Fruits of the Holy Spirit the demonstration through our actions that God is alive in us. Saint Paul lists the Fruits of the Holy Spirit in Galatians 5:22–23: love, joy, peace, patience, kindness, generosity, faithfulness, gentleness, and self-control. Church Tradition has added goodness, modesty, and chastity to make a total of 12.

Gifts of the Holy Spirit the permanent willingness, given to us by the Holy Spirit, that makes it possible for us to do what God asks of us. The Gifts of the Holy Spirit are drawn from Isaiah 11:1–3. They include wisdom, understanding, right judgment, courage, knowledge, and wonder and awe. Church Tradition has added reverence to make a total of seven.

ecumenism the movement among Christians that aims to restore unity to the Church founded by Jesus

faith a gift of God that helps us to believe in him. We profess our faith in the creed, celebrate it in the sacraments, live by it through our good conduct of loving God and our neighbor, and express it in prayer. It is a personal adherence of the whole person to God, who has revealed himself to us through words and actions throughout history.

fortitude the strength to choose to do the right thing even when that is difficult. Fortitude is one of the four central human virtues, called the cardinal virtues, by which we guide our conduct through faith and the use of reason. It is also one of the Gifts of the Holy Spirit, referred to as courage in the Rite of Confirmation.

holy one of the four Marks of the Church. It is the kind of life we live when we share in the life of God, who is all holiness. The Church is holy because it is united with Jesus Christ.

hope the confidence that God will always be with us, make us happy now and forever, and help us to live so that we will be with him forever

Immaculate Conception the belief that Mary was free from original sin from the moment of her conception. As the one chosen to be the mother of Jesus, whom the angel Gabriel addresses as "full of grace," Mary was redeemed from the moment of her conception. She is also the promise to us of the redemption to which we are all called.

infallible one of the traits of the Catholic Church given to it by the Holy Spirit whereby the pope is free from error when teaching on matters of faith or morals

justice the virtue that guides us to give to God and others what is due them. Justice is one of the four central human virtues, called the Cardinal Virtues, by which we guide our Christian life.

Kingdom of God God's rule over us, announced in the gospel and present in the Eucharist. The beginning of the Kingdom here on Earth is mysteriously present in the Church, and it will come in completeness at the end of time.

knowledge one of the seven Gifts of the Holy Spirit. This gift helps us to know what God asks of us and how we should respond.

Last Judgment the end of time as we know it, when Christ returns in glory. It will reveal the good that each person has done or failed to do. When Christ comes again we will know the meaning of God's plan and see how his goodness triumphs over the injustices committed by his creatures, and that in the end God's love is stronger than death.

Liturgy of the Eucharist the part of Mass in which the bread and wine are consecrated and become the Body and Blood of Jesus Christ, which we then receive in Holy Communion

Liturgy of the Word the part of the Mass in which we listen to God's Word from the Bible and consider what it means for us today. The Liturgy of the Word can also be a public prayer and proclamation of God's Word that is not followed by the Liturgy of the Eucharist.

magisterium the living, teaching office of the Church. This office, through the bishops and with the pope, provides an authentic interpretation of the Word of God. It ensures faithfulness to the teaching of the Apostles in matters of faith and morals.

Messiah a title that means "anointed one." It is from a Hebrew word that means the same thing as the Greek word Christ. "Messiah" is the title that was given to Jesus as priest, prophet, and king.

mortal sin a serious decision to turn away from God by doing something that we know is wrong. For a sin to be mortal it must be a very serious offense, the person must know how serious the sin is, and freely choose to do it anyway. Anyone who has freely chosen to turn away from God and dies before asking for forgiveness loses the chance of eternal life with God.

Nicene Creed the summary of Christian beliefs developed by the bishops at the first two councils of the Church, held in A.D. 325 and 381. It is the creed shared by most Christians, in the East and in the West.

one one of the four marks of the Church. The Church is one because of its source in the one God and because of its founder, Jesus Christ. Jesus, through his death on the cross, united all to God in one body. Within the unity of the Church there is great diversity because of the variety of the gifts given to its members.

original sin the consequence of the disobedience of the first human beings. They disobeyed God and chose to follow their own will rather than God's will. As a result, human beings lost the original blessing God had intended and became subject to sin and death. In Baptism we are restored to life with God through Jesus Christ, although we still experience the effects of original sin.

Particular Judgment our personal judgment by God at the moment of our death. We either accept or reject the grace of God while we're alive. When we die, our time for choosing is over and we will be judged on our love. We will be invited into the blessedness of God's presence if we have not chosen to reject it forever.

Paschal Mystery the work of salvation accomplished by Jesus Christ through his passion, death, and Resurrection. The Paschal Mystery is celebrated in the liturgy of the Church, and we experience its saving effects in the sacraments. In every liturgy of the Church, God the Father is blessed and adored as the source of all blessings we have received through his Son in order to make us his children through the Holy Spirit.

prudence the virtue that directs us toward good and helps us to choose the correct means to achieve that good. When we act with prudence, we carefully and thoughtfully consider our actions. Prudence is one of the cardinal moral virtues that guide our conscience and influence us to live according to the law of Christ.

purgatory a state of final cleansing after death of all the human imperfections of those who die in the friendship and grace of God to prepare them to enter the joy of God's presence in heaven

reverence one of the Gifts of the Holy Spirit which helps us love and worship God. It calls us to be faithful in our relationships with God and others. Reverence also helps us to be respectful and generous to others.

right judgment one of the Gifts of the Holy Spirit which helps us seek advice and be open to the advice of others. Right judgment also helps us give advice. It helps us to speak up and encourage others to do the right thing.

Rite of Christian Initiation of Adults the process that leads an adult who is not baptized to full initiation in the Catholic Church through the sacraments of Baptism, Confirmation, and the Eucharist

sacrament one of seven official rites through which God's life enters our lives in the liturgy through the work of the Holy Spirit. Christ's work in the liturgy is sacramental because his mystery is made present there by the power of the Holy Spirit. Jesus gave us three sacraments that bring us into the Church: Baptism, Confirmation, and the Eucharist. He gave us two sacraments that bring us healing: Penance and Anointing of the Sick. He also gave us two sacraments that help members serve the community: Matrimony and Holy Orders.

sanctifying grace the gift of God, given to us without our earning it, that introduces us to the intimacy of the Trinity, unites us with its life, and heals our human nature, wounded by sin. Sanctifying grace helps us respond to our vocation as God's adopted children, and it continues the work of making us holy that began at our Baptism.

spiritual works of mercy the kind acts through which we help our neighbors meet needs that are more than material. The spiritual works of mercy include instructing, advising, consoling, comforting, forgiving, and bearing wrongs with patience.

sponsor a practicing Catholic who presents a candidate for Baptism or Confirmation. The sponsor's duties are to support the candidate in living the faith and to exemplify the Christian life.

temperance the cardinal virtue that helps us to control our attraction to pleasure so that our natural desires are kept within proper limits. This moral virtue helps us choose to use created goods in moderation.

Ten Commandments the ten rules given by God to Moses on Mount Sinai that sum up God's law and show us what is required to love God and our neighbor. By following the Ten Commandments, the Hebrew people accepted their covenant with God.

theological virtues those virtues given us by God and not by human effort. They are faith, hope, and charity or love.

Torah the Hebrew word for "instruction" or "law." It is also the name of the first five books of the Old Testament: Genesis, Exodus, Leviticus, Numbers, and Deuteronomy.

Trinity the mystery of the existence of God in three Persons, the Father, the Son, and the Holy Spirit. Each Person is God, whole and entire. Each is distinct only in relationship of each to the others.

understanding one of the seven Gifts of the Holy Spirit. This gift helps us make the right choices in life and in our relationships with God and others.

venial sin a choice we make that weakens our relationship with God or other people. Venial sin wounds and lessens the divine life in us. If we make no effort to do better, venial sin can lead to more serious sin. Through our participation in the Eucharist, venial sin is forgiven when we are repentant, strengthening our relationship with God and others.

virtue an attitude or way of acting that enables us to do good

wisdom one of the seven Gifts of the Holy Spirit. Wisdom helps us to understand the purpose and plan of God and to live in a way that helps to bring about his plan. It begins in wonder and awe at God's greatness.

wonder and awe one of the seven Gifts of the Holy Spirit. Wonder and awe helps us recognize the greatness of God and our dependence on him. It leads us to marvel at God's incredible love for us.

1. I am the Lord Your God: you shall not have strange gods before me.
2. You shall not take the name of the Lord your God in vain.
3. Remember to keep holy the Lord's Day.
4. Honor your father and your mother.
5. You shall not kill.
6. You shall not commit adultery.
7. You shall not steal.
8. You shall not bear false witness against your neighbor.
9. You shall not covet your neighbor's wife.
10. You shall not covet your neighbor's goods.